# Test Your Vocabulary – Book 2

**Peter Watcyn-Jones**

**Illustrated by Sven Nordqvist**

PENGUIN BOOKS

PENGUIN BOOKS

Published by the Penguin Group
Penguin Books Ltd, 27 Wrights Lane, London W8 5TZ, England
Penguin Books USA Inc., 375 Hudson Street, New York, New York 10014, USA
Penguin Books Australia Ltd, Ringwood, Victoria, Australia
Penguin Books Canada Ltd, 10 Alcorn Avenue, Toronto, Ontario, Canada M4V 3B2
Penguin Books (NZ) Ltd, 182–190 Wairau Road, Auckland 10, New Zealand

Penguin Books Ltd, Registered Offices: Harmondsworth, Middlesex, England

First published in Sweden by Kursverksamhetens förlag 1979
Published in Penguin Books 1985
Revised edition published 1996
10 9 8 7 6 5 4 3

Text copyright © Peter Watcyn-Jones 1979
Illustrations copyright © Sven Nordqvist 1979
All rights reserved

Printed in England by Clays Ltd, St Ives plc
Set in Times

# CONTENTS

| | | |
|---|---|---|
| Introduction | | v |
| To the student | | v |
| Test | 1 Things in the home 1 | 1 |
| | 2 Synonyms – adjectives | 2 |
| | 3 Where do they live? | 3 |
| | 4 A true story | 4 |
| | 5 Things in the home 2 | 5 |
| | 6 Opposites – adjectives | 6 |
| | 7 Countries and nationalities | 7 |
| | 8 Quantities | 8 |
| | 9 Things in the home 3 | 9 |
| | 10 Choose the word 1 | 10 |
| | 11 Guess their jobs | 11 |
| | 12 The name of the room | 12 |
| | 13 Tools, etc. | 13 |
| | 14 Synonyms – verbs | 14 |
| | 15 Find the buildings | 15 |
| | 16 Word association 1 | 17 |
| | 17 Furniture and fittings 1 | 18 |
| | 18 Missing words – people's characteristics | 19 |
| | 19 Hobbies and pastimes | 20 |
| | 20 Prepositions 1 | 22 |
| | 21 Furniture and fittings 2 | 23 |
| | 22 Puzzle it out 1 – Who's who in Susan's family? | 24 |
| | 23 Animal sounds | 25 |
| | 24 Find the words | 26 |
| | 25 Newspaper misprints | 27 |
| | 26 Clothes | 28 |
| | 27 Choose the word 2 | 29 |
| | 28 Phrases | 30 |
| | 29 Complete the dialogue | 32 |
| | 30 Sports, games, pastimes – equipment | 34 |
| Test | 31 Where do you find them? | 35 |
| | 32 Choose the answer | 36 |
| | 33 The sea-shore | 38 |
| | 34 Prepositions 2 | 39 |
| | 35 Parts of a car | 40 |
| | 36 Add a letter | 41 |
| | 37 Cartoons | 42 |
| | 38 Too many words | 44 |
| | 39 British and American English | 45 |
| | 40 Puzzle it out 2 – Who's who at the party? | 46 |
| | 41 Confusing words | 48 |
| | 42 Opposites – verbs | 50 |
| | 43 Classifications | 51 |
| | 44 Types of transport | 52 |
| | 45 Synonyms – more adjectives | 53 |
| | 46 From Bear to Coat | 54 |
| | 47 Bits and pieces 1 | 55 |
| | 48 Missing words – books, etc. | 56 |
| | 49 Word association 2 | 58 |
| | 50 Bits and pieces 2 | 59 |
| | 51 Missing words – adverbs | 60 |
| | 52 Anagrams | 62 |
| | 53 What's the verb? | 64 |
| | 54 Choose the word 3 | 66 |
| | 55 Right or wrong? | 68 |
| | 56 Choose the adjective | 70 |
| | 57 What's the rhyming word? | 71 |
| | 58 Same word – different meaning | 72 |
| | 59 Words with silent letters | 74 |
| | 60 Adjective + noun combinations | 76 |
| | Answers | 77 |

# INTRODUCTION

Nowadays few people will dispute the importance of vocabulary, especially the need for active vocabulary practice. The *Test Your Vocabulary* books filled this need when they first came out, and they continue to do so. There are six books in the series, from elementary to advanced level. In this new edition of the series each book has ten new tests. To facilitate self-study there is a full Answer Key. Students using *Test Your Vocabulary* will find learning vocabulary both stimulating and enjoyable.

*Test Your Vocabulary 2* is the third book in the series and is intended for intermediate students. There are sixty tests, and approximately 1,000 words in the book. The tests cover areas of vocabulary such as jobs, clothes and people's characteristics. There are twelve picture tests on everyday objects found in the home, furniture and parts of a car. Finally, there are tests on synonyms, antonyms, prepositions, British and American English, anagrams, adverbs, adjective–noun collocations, rhyming words and words with more than one meaning.

# TO THE STUDENT

This book will help you to learn a lot of new English words. But in order for the new words to become 'fixed' in your mind, you need to test yourself again and again. Here is one method you can use to help you learn the words.

1   Read through the instructions carefully for the test you are going to try. Then try the test, writing your answers **in pencil**.
2   When you have finished, check your answers and correct any mistakes you have made. Read through the test again, paying special attention to the words you didn't know or got wrong.
3   Try the test again five minutes later. You can do this either by covering up the words (for example, in the picture tests) or by asking a friend to test you. Repeat this until you can remember all the words.
4   **Rub out your answers.**
5   Try the test again the following day. (You should remember most of the words.)
6   Finally, plan to try the test at least twice again within the following month. After this most of the words will be 'fixed' in your mind.

# 1 Things in the home 1

Write the number of each drawing next to the correct word.

| | |
|---|---|
| coat hanger | 12 |
| potato peeler | . . . . . |
| lightbulb | . . . . . |
| colander | . . . . . |
| broom | . . . . . |
| plate | . . . . . |
| egg slicer | . . . . . |
| dustpan | . . . . . |
| carpet beater | . . . . . |
| scrubbing brush | . . . . . |
| cheese slicer | . . . . . |
| tea towel | . . . . . |

# 2 Synonyms – adjectives

Give a synonym for each of the words in brackets in the following sentences. Choose from the ones below. Number 1 has been done for you.

| | | | |
|---|---|---|---|
| odd | bashful | attractive | authentic |
| cheeky | enjoyable | unbelievable | obstinate |
| enormous | ample | big-headed | appalling |
| hilarious | vital | keen | |

1  He was one of the most (good-looking) *attractive* men she had ever seen.

2  We had a really (pleasant) ................................. time in Brighton last week.

3  David is always telling people how good he is at everything. He's so (conceited) ..............................

4  The play last night was (terrible) ................................. At least half the audience walked out in the middle of it.

5  There's something very (peculiar) ................................. about Mr Brown's behaviour today. Haven't you noticed?

6  Have you seen James and Sally's new house? It's really (huge) .............. ..........................

7  He won't take my advice. He's so (stubborn) .................................

8  I was always very (shy) ................................. as a child and hated going to parties or meeting new people.

9  My son loves school. In fact, in some ways he's too (enthusiastic) ................... ................ I mean, it's the only thing he ever talks about.

10  It looked like (a genuine) an ................................. Picasso, but in fact it was only a copy.

11  I think Martha is going to have a lot of problems with her children. They're so (rude) ................................. to everyone.

12  You should have done it by now. You've had (sufficient) ............................. time.

13  You must read this story – it's quite (incredible) ................................. !

14  Hard work and ambition are (essential) ................................. if you want to get on in life.

15  You must go and see the new "Monty Python" film – it's (very funny) .................................

# 3 Where do they live?

Read through the following sentences and fill in the missing words.

1 Most English families live in a  . . . . .
2 A king lives in a  . . . . . . . . . . . . . . . . .
3 A monk lives in a  . . . . . . . . . . . . . .
4 A nun lives in a  . . . . . . . . . . . . . . . .
5 Soldiers live in a  . . . . . . . . . . . . . . . .
6 A prisoner lives in a  . . . . . . . . . . . . .
7 A gipsy lives in a  . . . . . . . . . . . . . . . .
8 An eskimo lives in an  . . . . . . . . . . . . .
9 A bee lives in a  . . . . . . . . . . . . . . . . .
10 A bird lives in a  . . . . . . . . . . . . . . . . .
11 A dog lives in a  . . . . . . . . . . . . . . . . .
12 A horse lives in a  . . . . . . . . . . . . . . . .
13 A pig lives in a  . . . . . . . . . . . . . . . . . .
14 A spider lives in a  . . . . . . . . . . . . . . .
15 An eagle lives in an  . . . . . . . . . . . . . .

3

# 4 A true story

Look at the following cartoon-strip of something that really happened. Then try to work out which sentence goes with which drawing. Number the sentences 1–10. Number 1 has been done for you.

**A TRUE STORY**

(   ) Somehow the bees made a hole in the paper and climbed up the man's legs.

(   ) Officials noticed a man without trousers and thought he was an escaped lunatic.

(   ) To avoid being stung by the bees, he explained his dilemma to the women in the compartment, who left.

(   ) They wrapped round the neck of a ticket inspector, who was attacked by the bees.

( **1** ) A few years ago, a Hungarian was travelling by train to Budapest.

(   ) It took the bee expert three days to convince doctors at the Mental Hospital that he was sane.

(   ) He took off his trousers – and an express train travelling in the opposite direction set up such a draught that his trousers flew out into the corridor.

(   ) He was arrested and put in a strait-jacket.

(   ) He had some bees in a milk bottle which was covered with brown paper.

(   ) Someone pulled the communication cord, the train pulled up and caught fire.

4

# 5 Things in the home 2

Write the number of each drawing next to the correct word.

pepper mill .....
liquidizer/blender .....
fire guard .....
bowl .....
tray .....
briefcase .....
lemon squeezer .....
tea strainer .....
bellows .....
bottle opener .....
suitcase .....
ladle .....

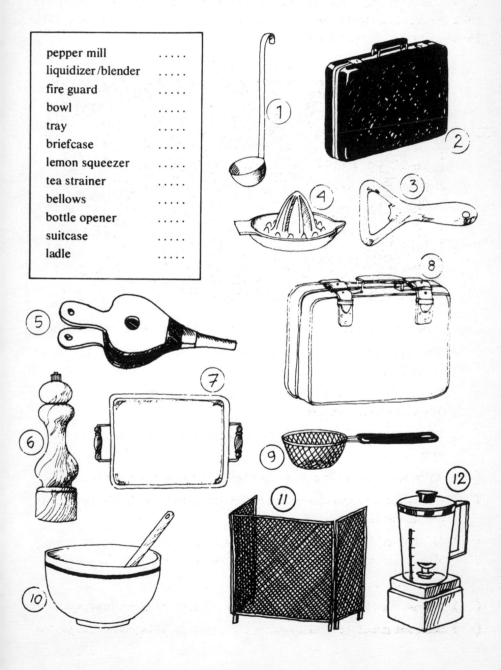

5

# 6 Opposites – adjectives

Find the opposites of the words on the left. Choose from the ones on the right. Number 1 has been done for you.

| ADJECTIVE | OPPOSITE |
|---|---|
| 1 harmless | *harmful* |
| 2 generous | ................................. |
| 3 permanent | ................................. |
| 4 industrious | ................................. |
| 5 gigantic | ................................. |
| 6 friendly | ................................. |
| 7 dull | ................................. |
| 8 daring | ................................. |
| 9 dear | ................................. |
| 10 narrow-minded | ................................. |
| 11 real | ................................. |
| 12 horrible | ................................. |
| 13 gradual | ................................. |
| 14 keen | ................................. |
| 15 fortunate | ................................. |

lazy
broad-minded
timid
sudden
unfortunate
mean
wonderful
hostile
temporary
uninterested
exciting
cheap
imaginary
harmful
minute

# 7 Countries and nationalities

Fill in the following crossword and see how many countries and nationalities you can remember.

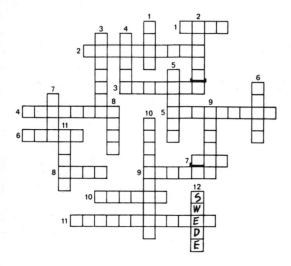

## DOWN

1 This person has no trouble buying petrol.
2 The river Ganges flows through this country.
3 This person lives in a country near France, where they speak two languages.
4 This person lives in a country whose capital is Prague.
5 They play a lot of ice-hockey in this country.
6 ......... people make very good bankers.
7 A native of Poland.
8 A very famous .........is Victor Borge.
9 Both Iraq and Iran border this country.
10 These people live in south-east Asia.
11 A country with a famous canal.
12 See above .........

## ACROSS

1 A native of one of the countries of Scandinavia.
2 A small country whose capital is Wellington.
3 They grow tulips in this country.
4 One of the countries of Gt. Britain.
5 Both an island and a continent.
6 The bazouki is a typical .........instrument.
7 This person suffered a lot under Hitler.
8 A country in South America.
9 A country full of fjords.
10 This person loves cold weather.
11 Large country in North America.

# 8 Quantities

Fill in the correct phrase under each drawing.

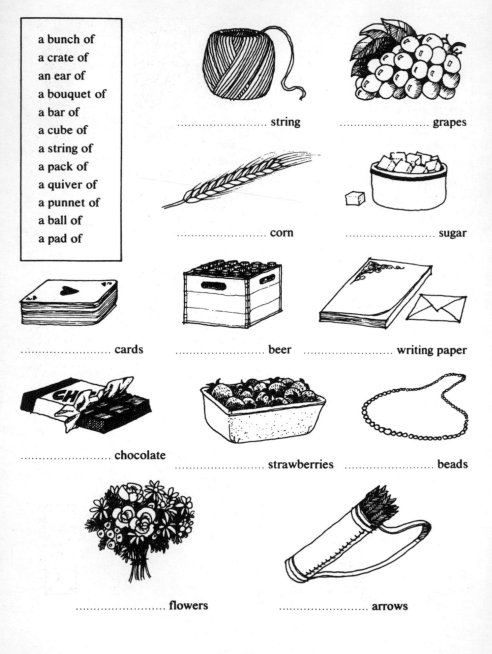

a bunch of
a crate of
an ear of
a bouquet of
a bar of
a cube of
a string of
a pack of
a quiver of
a punnet of
a ball of
a pad of

........................ string

........................ grapes

........................ corn

........................ sugar

........................ cards

........................ beer

........................ writing paper

........................ chocolate

........................ strawberries

........................ beads

........................ flowers

........................ arrows

# 9 Things in the home 3

Write the number of each drawing next to the correct word.

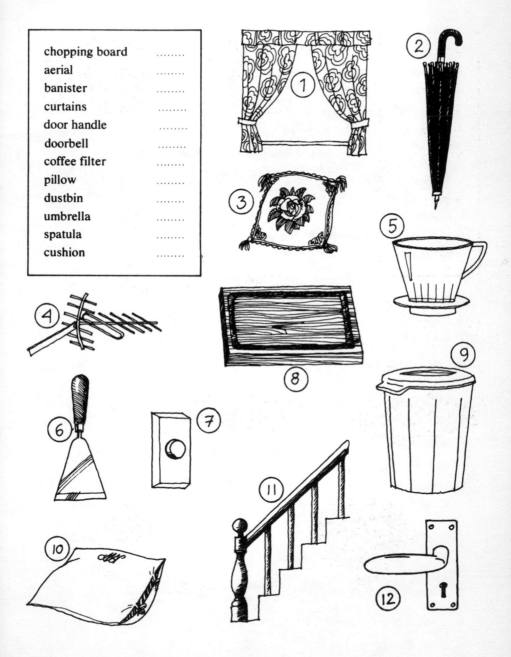

chopping board ........
aerial ........
banister ........
curtains ........
door handle ........
doorbell ........
coffee filter ........
pillow ........
dustbin ........
umbrella ........
spatula ........
cushion ........

# 10 Choose the word 1

Choose the word which best completes each sentence.

1 A bed on board a ship is called a ................
   a sleeper       b cabin       c bunk       d dormitory

2 I have no brothers or sisters. I am ................. child.
   a an only       b a sole       c a unique       d a single

3 I'm terribly sorry, I seem to have ............... my book at home.
   a lost       b forgotten       c left       d hidden

4 My sister and I are always quarrelling. We just don't seem to ...............
   a get off       b get together       c get on       d get by

5 Most parents find it difficult to ............... their children nowadays.
   a grow up       b foster       c develop       d bring up

6 I ............... to inform you that your mother died ten minutes ago.
   a sorry       b regret       c apologise       d pity

7 I think everyone should ............... the Human Rights movement.
   a agree       b support       c stand up       d supply

8 I only paid £3 for this dress. It was a real ...............
   a find       b sale       c bargain       d cheap

9 I always try to ............... something each month for my holidays.
   a save       b spare       c spend       d put

10 I don't have a job. I'm ...............
   a lonely       b sick       c unused       d unemployed

11 Which horse shall we ............... on in the 2.15 race?
   a back       b bet       c place       d win

12 Manchester United ............... Liverpool in the F.A. Cup Final.
   a beat       b won       c sailed       d lost

# 11 Guess their jobs

Read through the following sentences and then write down which job each of the following people have.

| 1. MISS REES | 2. MR BERRY | 3. MR. GUARD | 4. MRS. KNOWLES | 5. MR TRAIN |
|---|---|---|---|---|
| 6. MRS PLOD | 7. MRS CARTER | 8. MR AUSTIN | 9. MR FIELD | 10. MISS SAYER |

1 You go to this person when you want to take out some money at a bank.
2 This person helps you when you play golf by carrying your clubs and giving you advice.
3. This person looks after a block of flats or an office.
4. When you have a legal problem, you can always go to this person.
5. He carries your bags for you at the station.
6. This person delivers letters.
7 This person performs operations at a hospital.
8 If you have a lot of money, you might employ this person to drive you around.
9 This person keeps animals and grows crops.
10 If you have a problem with your speech, this person can help you overcome it.

Miss Rees is a c . . . . . . . . . . . . . . . . . . . . . .     Mrs Plod is a p . . . . . . . . . . . . . . . . . . . . . .
Mr Berry is a c . . . . . . . . . . . . . . . . . . . . . .     Mrs Carter is a s . . . . . . . . . . . . . . . . . . . . . .
Mr Guard is a c . . . . . . . . . . . . . . . . . . . . . .     Mr Austin is a c . . . . . . . . . . . . . . . . . . . . . .
Miss Knowles is a s . . . . . . . . . . . . . . . . . .     Mr Field is a f . . . . . . . . . . . . . . . . . . . . . . .
Mr Train is a p . . . . . . . . . . . . . . . . . . . . . .     Miss Sayer is a s . . . . . . . . t . . . . . . . . . .

# 12   The name of the room

Read through the sentences and fill in the missing words.

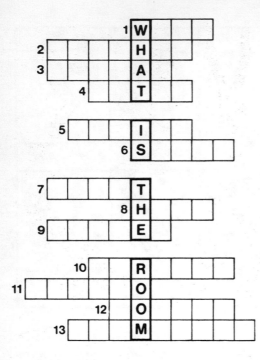

1 A room in a hospital where people needing treatment stay.

2 A room in a house or flat where you usually do the cooking.

3 A room under a house.

4 A room at the top of a house, under the roof. It is often used for storing things.

5 Small rooms on board a ship where the crew and passengers sleep.

6 A room used for studying or working.

7 A room under a church.

8 The part of a ship below deck where goods are stored.

9 A room in a house where food is stored.

10 A room in a house used by a family for receiving guests – a sort of "best room".
(It is not so common nowadays.)

11 A room where an artist or photographer works.

12 A large, comfortable room for sitting, found at a hotel.

13 A room with lots of beds used for sleeping, e.g. at a boarding school.

# 13 Tools, etc.

Write the number of each drawing next to the correct word.

| | |
|---|---|
| plane | . . . . . |
| file | . . . . . |
| axe | . . . . . |
| pliers | . . . . . |
| extension cable | . . . . . |
| jack | . . . . . |
| secateurs | . . . . . |
| watering can | . . . . . |
| sickle | . . . . . |
| vice | . . . . . |
| fire extinguisher | . . . . . |
| chisel | . . . . . |

# 14 Synonyms – verbs

Give a synonym for each of the words in brackets in the following sentences. Choose from the ones below. (Make any other necessary changes.) Number 1 has been done for you.

| | | | |
|---|---|---|---|
| detest | purchase | spoil | trip |
| inform | accomplish | put off | alter |
| enter | moan | recollect | occur |
| brag | vanish | scare | |

1 Being a gentleman, I allowed the women to (go in) *enter* first.

2 They were all watching the U.F.O. when it suddenly (disappeared) ....................
   ....................

3 This is something I (bought) .................................... from an antique dealer in Chelsea.

4 I love watching football, but my wife (loathes) .................................... it.

5 He (stumbled) .................................... and fell as he was leaving the church.

6 You won't (achieve) .................................... anything if you don't work harder.

7 The manuscript is basically good – but there are still parts of it that need to be (changed) ....................................

8 I couldn't (remember) .................................... where I had first met her.

9 The match has been (postponed) .................................... until next week.

10 Alfred Hitchcock's films really (frighten) .................................... me; especially the one he made about a lot of birds attacking people.

11 Bad weather completely (ruined) .................................... the Garden Party.

12 I don't like the new secretary very much – she's always (complaining) .................................... about something or other.

13 Can you tell me in your own words exactly what (happened) ....................?

14 Would you please (notify) .................................... me the moment Miss Baker gets back?

15 I can't stand Doreen. She's always (boasting) .................................... about the places she's been to.

# 15 Find the buildings

On the following map are ten buildings. Read through the information below and then write down the names of the various buildings.

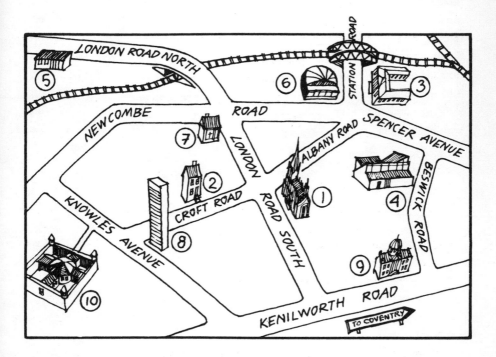

Building number 1 is always full on Sundays.

The Local Council meet once a week at the building in Kenilworth Road.

The building near the railway bridge is full of old things, including the skeleton of a dinosaur.

Building number 8 is very high.

Building number 10 is surrounded by walls 20 feet high.

If you are looking for a house or a flat you should go to Croft Road.

When driving from Coventry, take the second turning on the right to get to St. Mary's.

There's a Van Gogh Exhibition on this week in Beswick Road.

They're showing "Star Wars" at the building at the corner of Newcombe Road and Station Road.

When my father died we ordered a coffin from the building in London Road South. The building at the corner of Croft Road and Knowles Avenue is divided into offices. Building number 5 is where you can go to put a bet on a horse.

Building number 1 is a ................................................................

Building number 2 is an ........................................... (2 words)

Building number 3 is a ................................................................

Building number 4 is an ........................................... (2 words)

Building number 5 is a ........................................... (2 words)

Building number 6 is a ................................................................

Building number 7 is an ................................................................

Building number 8 is an ........................................... (2 words)

Building number 9 is the ........................................... (2 words)

Building number 10 is a ................................................................

# 16 Word association 1

Each of the following groups of four words is in some way connected with the same thing. Write down this word for each of the groups. Number 1 has been done for you.

1 clutch, motorway, drive, Volvo

2 referee, penalty, corner, Leeds

3 percussion, symphony, conductor, violins

4 petal, stem, rose, garden

5 collar, tail, bark, Alsatian

6 bride, ring, church, photographer

7 kitchen, stairs, family, address

8 string, Segovia, fret, chord

9 pillow, night, mattress, snore

10 telescope, Venus, galaxy, science

11 gun, war, fight, uniform

12 waveband, transistor, aerial, tuner

13 key, letter, secretary, ribbon

14 landlord, glass, darts, bar

15 umpire, net, set, court

16 eat, potatoes, lunch, cook

17 bank, Danube, flow, estuary

18 heel, lace, sole, wear

19 matron, ward, patient, illness

20 crotchet, compose, treble clef, classical

# 17 Furniture and fittings 1

Write the number of each drawing next to the correct word.

stove (cooker) . . . . .
washing machine . . . . .
fridge . . . . .
coffee table . . . . .
bedside table . . . . .
shower . . . . .
bath . . . . .
wardrobe . . . . .
broom cupboard . . . . .
fluorescent light . . . . .
oil lamp . . . . .
ceiling light . . . . .

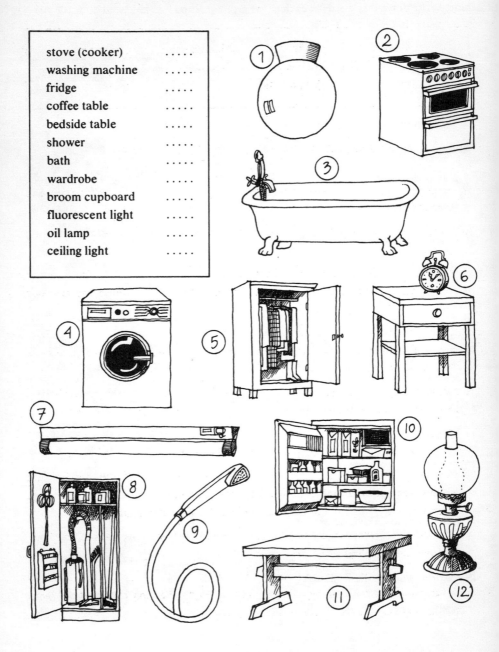

# 18 Missing words – people's characteristics

Put the following words in the correct sentences.

| | | | |
|---|---|---|---|
| ambitious | big-headed | intelligent | immature |
| rude | obstinate | moody | eccentric |
| strict | sympathetic | | |

1 John is always telling people how well he plays the guitar. He's so ......................
................

2 Many girls of 16 and 17 are far too .................................... to get married and have children.

3 I see Clive's passed all his exams again. It must be wonderful to be so ..............
.....................

4 The trouble with Jane is that she's so .................................... One minute she's laughing, the next she's sulking. You just don't know where you are with her.

5 One of the things I like about Pamela is that she's so ....................................
If you have a problem you know you can go to her and that she'll listen to you and try to help all she can.

6 Mrs Green's children are so .................................... They never say "Please" or "Thank you" and only last week I heard them swearing at the postman.

7 My son's very .................................... He doesn't want to work in an office all his life. In fact he keeps telling me that one day he's going to be Prime Minister.

8 My uncle is very .................................... No matter what the weather, he always wears a bright red cape when he goes out and a matching pair of boots. Everyone stares at him, but he doesn't mind. He likes being different.

9 My husband never sees my point of view. He has his opinions and nothing I say will ever change them. He's so ....................................

10 When I was a teenager, my father was very .................................... He'd never allow me to wear make-up or have a boyfriend, and if I went out with friends I always had to be home by 10 o'clock.

# 19 Hobbies and pastimes

Fill in the following crossword. Each answer is a hobby or pastime.

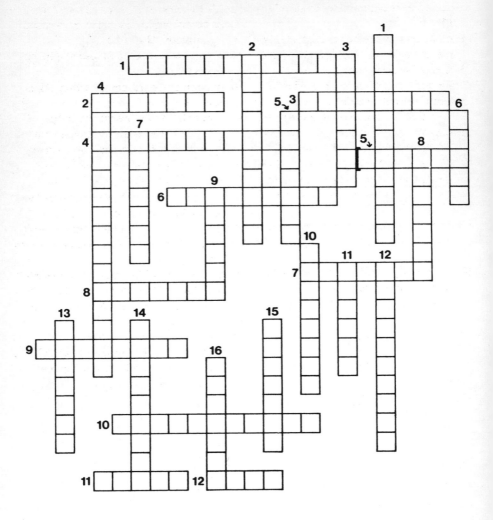

## ACROSS

1 An outdoor activity for those who like running and map reading.
2 Not on land.
3 A useful activity which some people can do at the same time as watching TV.
4 An interest in the ancient world. May spend weekends digging somewhere.
5 A popular card game.
6 An activity which is never finished. Can't be done in a flat.
7 You need a loom to do this properly.
8 A good way to spend the weekend. But not as comfortable as a hotel!
9 A creative hobby. You may even sell one or two of the things you create.
10 An indoor game for 2–4 players. (2 words)
11 Most people are interested in this whether they play an instrument or not.
12 A relaxing activity. You may spend hours on your head!

## DOWN

1 All you need is a camera.
2 A relaxing activity, mainly done by women. Could be called painting with wool, nylon, etc.
3 It's the closest thing to being a bird.
4 A hobby which can also be a good investment. (2 words)
5 A good way to keep fit and of getting around.
6 A popular board game. Often takes hours.
7 A popular hobby where the thing you make disappears once you make it.
8 If you do this then you'll know how to do the rumba, samba, etc.
9 You need an animal to do this.
10 A popular summer pastime – especially when the weather is warm.
11 A pastime for those who fancy themselves as Richard Burton and Elizabeth Taylor.
12 A winter pastime. Can be done indoors or out-of-doors. (2 words)
13 A famous Chinese game, played with tiles. (2 words)
14 An indoor game with balls.
15 A relaxing, outdoor hobby where you sit for hours before anything happens.
16 A creative hobby using clay.

# 20 Prepositions 1

Put in the missing prepositions in the following sentences.

1 I'm very disappointed ................ him.
   a  on            b  in            c  of

2 Who else was ................ the party on Saturday?
   a  at            b  on            c  to

3 He had difficulty ................ starting the car.
   a  with          b  to            c  in

4 What do English people eat ................ Christmas?
   a  to            b  at            c  under

5 That music was written ................ Beethoven.
   a  of            b  with          c  by

6 I'm very conscious ................ my big nose.
   a  of            b  at            c  with

7 The police car chased the robbers ................ the streets.
   a  among         b  in            c  through

8 I'm looking ................ my lighter. Have you seen it?
   a  to            b  after          c  for

9 I haven't smoked ................ ages.
   a  for           b  since          c  at

10 I'm tired ................ learning English.
   a  on            b  of            c  with

11 Here – divide this bar of chocolate ................ yourselves.
   a  in            b  among          c  with

12 His opinion differs ................ mine.
   a  to            b  from           c  with

13 You go on – there's no need to wait ................ me.
   a  on            b  by            c  for

14 If you don't know what a word means, you can always look it ................ in a
   dictionary.
   a  on            b  over           c  up

15 He was very proud ................ being English.
   a  of            b  over           c  with

22

# 21 Furniture and fittings 2

Write the number of each drawing next to the correct word.

shaving socket . . . . .
record storage unit . . . . .
time switch . . . . .
window sill . . . . .
fan heater . . . . .
trolley . . . . .
room divider . . . . .
door knob . . . . .
extractor fan . . . . .
curtain rail . . . . .
coat stand . . . . .
window box . . . . .

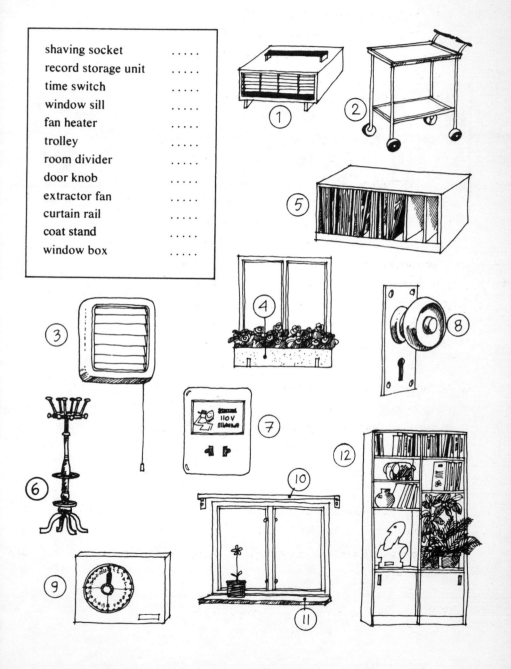

# 22 Puzzle it out 1 – Who's who in Susan's family?

Read through the sentences below, then see if you can work out the relationship between the various people and Susan.

BILL   TED   ANNE   FREDA   OLIVE   PAUL

Bill is Ted's father.
Freda is Olive's daughter.
Anne's husband has a beard.
Paul is Ted's brother-in-law.
Olive is Bill's sister.
Susan's father wears glasses.

Bill is Susan's        .........................
Ted is Susan's         .........................
Anne is Susan's        .........................
Freda is Susan's       .........................
Olive is Susan's       .........................
Paul is Susan's        .........................

# 23 Animal sounds

Fill in the correct verb under each drawing.

lows
barks
trumpets
croaks
neighs
bleats
roars
squeaks
grunts
crows

a pig . . . . . . . . . . . . . . .

a dog . . . . . . . . . . . . . . .

a mouse . . . . . . . . . . . . . . .

a cock . . . . . . . . . . . . . . .

a frog . . . . . . . . . . . . . . .

an elephant . . . . . . . . . . . . . . .

a horse . . . . . . . . . . . . . . .

a lamb . . . . . . . . . . . . . . .

a lion . . . . . . . . . . . . . . .

a cow . . . . . . . . . . . . . . .

# 24 Find the words

Fill in the missing first and last letters in the words below. A clue is given for each word.

| # | | | | | | Clue |
|---|---|---|---|---|---|---|
| 1 | | H | R | O | A | | part of the body |
| 2 | | A | T | U | R | | a planet |
| 3 | | A | L | L | E | | a container for money |
| 4 | | A | B | B | I | | an animal |
| 5 | | A | U | C | E | | a piece of crockery |
| 6 | | P | I | D | E | | an insect |
| 7 | | I | L | L | O | | a tree |
| 8 | | A | L | M | O | | a fish |
| 9 | | A | N | I | S | | to disappear |
| 10 | | L | O | U | S | | a piece of clothing |
| 11 | | K | I | I | N | | a sport |
| 12 | | I | G | H | T | | a number |
| 13 | | I | G | E | O | | a bird |
| 14 | | A | W | Y | E | | a job |
| 15 | | U | I | T | A | | a musical instrument |
| 16 | | E | P | H | E | | a relative |
| 17 | | I | Z | A | R | | a reptile |
| 18 | | A | D | I | S | | a vegetable |
| 19 | | E | T | R | O | | Americans call it gasoline |
| 20 | | U | T | T | E | | a pipe at the bottom of a roof to carry away rainwater |

# 25 Newspaper misprints

In each of the following extracts from a newspaper there is a misprint. Write down the word which is wrong and also write down which word should have been used instead.

|  | Misprint | Correct word |
|---|---|---|
| 1 He is now being kept alive by an artificial respirator and huge doses of rugs. | *rugs* | *drugs* |
| 2 The route taken by the King and Queen was lined by clapping, cheering crows. | . . . . . . . . . . . . . . | . . . . . . . . . . . . . . |
| 3 Barry Jones was seriously burnt last weekend when he came in contact with a high voltage wife. | . . . . . . . . . . . . . . | . . . . . . . . . . . . . . |
| 4 Congratulations and best wishes to my daring fiancée on her 21st birthday. | . . . . . . . . . . . . . . | . . . . . . . . . . . . . . |
| 5 He was taken to hospital with heard injuries. | . . . . . . . . . . . . . . | . . . . . . . . . . . . . . |
| 6 Young lady required for publishing company. Previous experience not essential bust must be able to type. | . . . . . . . . . . . . . . | . . . . . . . . . . . . . . |
| 7 1969 Volvo. One owner. God. Low mileage. | . . . . . . . . . . . . . . | . . . . . . . . . . . . . . |
| 8 A neighbour also claims to have seen the ghost and it upset him so much that he has not eaten property for several days. | . . . . . . . . . . . . . . | . . . . . . . . . . . . . . |
| 9 The bank robbers tried to escape but were cornered by a polite dog. | . . . . . . . . . . . . . . | . . . . . . . . . . . . . . |
| 10 Heat a very small amount of oil in a frying pan. Fry meatballs, burning them as they cook for about 15 minutes. | . . . . . . . . . . . . . . | . . . . . . . . . . . . . . |

# 26 Clothes

Write the number of each drawing next to the correct word.

| | |
|---|---|
| bow tie | ..... |
| bowler hat | ..... |
| beret | ..... |
| cardigan | ..... |
| sweater | ..... |
| apron | ..... |
| gloves | ..... |
| braces | ..... |
| clogs | ..... |
| shorts | ..... |
| sandals | ..... |
| string vest | ..... |

# 27 Choose the word 2

Choose the word which best completes each sentence.

1 My work's got worse and worse. Unless I ................. I'll fail my exams in the summer.
   a  get well        b  improve        c  increase        d  get back

2 Oh dear! My watch has .................!
   a  ended           b  stopped        c  finished        d  completed

3 If you work for someone, then you are .................
   a  a slave         b  unemployed     c  an employer     d  an employee

4 I'm afraid there's no ................. of seeing Mr Brown until tomorrow.
   a  possibility     b  wish           c  opportunity     d  chance

5 The ................. around this town is quite beautiful.
   a  countryside     b  scene          c  nature          d  country

6 He's always telling me what to do. He's so .................
   a  cruel           b  bossy          c  helpful         d  charming

7 His parents gave him everything he asked for. He was thoroughly ......................
   a  disturbed       b  ashamed        c  full up         d  spoilt

8 I still feel like a cigarette even though I ................. smoking two years ago.
   a  gave in         b  gave up        c  gave over       d  completed

9 He wants to get to the top before he is thirty. He is very .................
   a  tall            b  ambitious      c  intelligent     d  industrial

10 John always arrives on time. He's so .................
   a  careful         b  boring         c  punctual        d  timeless

11 She made the ................. mistake of forgetting to put the ''s'' on the verb in the third person singular.
   a  classic         b  important      c  classical       d  famous

12 I was very ................. for all the advice she gave me.
   a  glad            b  grateful       c  in debt         d  pleased

# 28 Phrases

Fill in the missing words in the following drawings. Choose an appropriate phrase from the ones below:

| | |
|---|---|
| a Yes, I think so. | g How about going to the pictures? |
| b Yes, that would be nice. | h No, there's no need, thanks. |
| c Yes, very funny. | i No, not just now, thanks. |
| d Not at all. | j It was great fun. |
| e No, I don't think I have. | k No, not very. |
| f Yes – do help yourself. | l That's rubbish! |

31

# 29 Complete the dialogue

In the following dialogue, the part of Paul has been left out. Put in the words he speaks in the right order from the phrases below.

---

- About a month ago.
- St. Richard's Comprehensive?
- Well, as a matter of fact, we've decided to get a divorce.
- Oh, sorry!
- (Laughing) I see. Still the same old John. You haven't changed a bit!
- Yes, that's right. Sweden.
- You must enjoy it there, then.
- Oh, I live here now.
- No, only me.
- Ah well, it can't be helped. And there aren't any children fortunately.
- John! This is a surprise!
- But anyway, enough of me. What are you doing these days?

---

Paul: .................................................................

John: That's all right.

Paul: .................................................................

John: Paul! Paul Jennings! Well I never! What on earth are you doing here?

Paul: .................................................................

John: Do you? But the last I heard of you, you were teaching abroad somewhere.

Paul: .................................................................

John: So when did you come back?

Paul: .................................................................

John: And is Sally with you?

Paul: .................................................................

John: Only you?

Paul: .................................................................

John: Oh, I am sorry to hear that, Paul.

Paul: .................................................................

John: Yes, that's one blessing, I suppose.

Paul: ............................................................

John: Oh, still teaching, you know. Same school as before.

Paul: ............................................................

John: That's the one.

Paul: ............................................................

John: Well, let's just say it helps pay the rent, shall we?

Paul: ............................................................

John: No, neither have you. I'd have recognised you anywhere.

# 30 Sports, games, pastimes – equipment

Write the number of each drawing next to the correct word or words.

| | |
|---|---|
| dartboard | . . . . . |
| tennis racquet | . . . . . |
| badminton racquet | . . . . . |
| air pistol | . . . . . |
| golf club | . . . . . |
| tent | . . . . . |
| chess set | . . . . . |
| dice | . . . . . |
| figure skate | . . . . . |
| ski stick | . . . . . |
| shin pad | . . . . . |
| dumbbell | . . . . . |
| shuttlecock | . . . . . |
| binoculars | . . . . . |
| ice hockey stick | . . . . . |

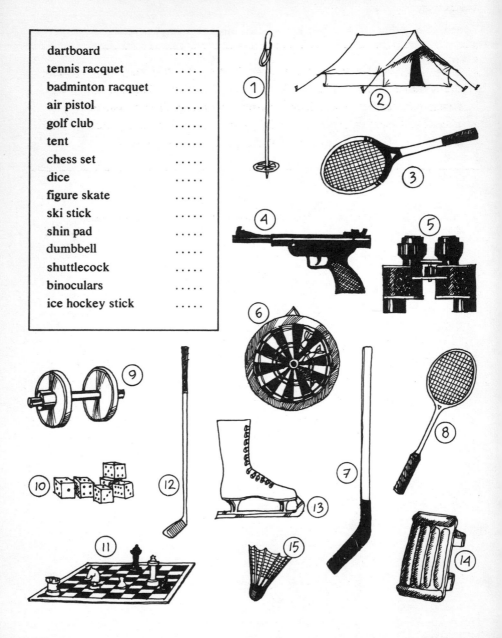

# 31 Where do you find them?

Here are 40 words arranged in alphabetical order. Work out where you are most likely to find them and write them down under the appropriate words. (There are five words under each.)

aisle, altar, blackboard, boot, bumper, button, clutch, collar, congregation, crew, cutlery, date stamp, deck, desks, dishwasher, filing cabinet, fridge, frying pan, funnel, horn, lapel, matron, operating theatre, patients, pew, playground, pocket, portholes, pulpit, pupils, rails, seatbelt, secretary, sink unit, sleeve, staffroom, stapler, stethoscope, typewriter, ward.

1 in a school
. . . . . . . . . . . . . .
. . . . . . . . . . . . . .
. . . . . . . . . . . . . .
. . . . . . . . . . . . . .
. . . . . . . . . . . . . .

2 in the kitchen
. . . . . . . . . . . . . .
. . . . . . . . . . . . . .
. . . . . . . . . . . . . .
. . . . . . . . . . . . . .
. . . . . . . . . . . . . .

3 on a boat
. . . . . . . . . . . . . .
. . . . . . . . . . . . . .
. . . . . . . . . . . . . .
. . . . . . . . . . . . . .
. . . . . . . . . . . . . .

4 in a church
. . . . . . . . . . . . . .
. . . . . . . . . . . . . .
. . . . . . . . . . . . . .
. . . . . . . . . . . . . .
. . . . . . . . . . . . . .

5 on a jacket
. . . . . . . . . . . . . .
. . . . . . . . . . . . . .
. . . . . . . . . . . . . .
. . . . . . . . . . . . . .
. . . . . . . . . . . . . .

6 in a hospital
. . . . . . . . . . . . . .
. . . . . . . . . . . . . .
. . . . . . . . . . . . . .
. . . . . . . . . . . . . .
. . . . . . . . . . . . . .

7 in an office
. . . . . . . . . . . . . .
. . . . . . . . . . . . . .
. . . . . . . . . . . . . .
. . . . . . . . . . . . . .
. . . . . . . . . . . . . .

8 on a car
. . . . . . . . . . . . . .
. . . . . . . . . . . . . .
. . . . . . . . . . . . . .
. . . . . . . . . . . . . .
. . . . . . . . . . . . . .

# 32 Choose the answer

Choose the correct answer for each of the following.

1 The words attic, skylight and porch all have something to do with:

   a  a theatre      b  painting      c  a house      d  sport

   e  cars

2 Which of these is not right?

   a  a bunch of bananas         d  a dozen eggs

   b  a box of matches           e  a bar of chocolate

   c  a steak of meat

3 If a person is conceited, he or she is:

   a  careful              d  suspicious

   b  shy                 e  crazy

   c  big-headed

4 This is:

   a  a safety pin

   b  a paperclip

   c  a drawing pin

   d  a stapler

   e  a nail

5 A trunk is part of:

   a  a knife            d  a telephone

   b  a tree            e  a television

   c  a flower

6 Which of the following would help you see distant objects more clearly?

   a  spectacles        d  a cheek

   b  a telegraph      e  binoculars

   c  a microscope

7 What is the opposite of rude?

  a  certain

  b  impolite

  c  clean

  d  courteous

  e  successful

8 Where would you find a sole?

  a  on a shoe

  b  on a skirt

  c  on a shirt

  d  on a jacket

  e  on a hat

9 To be "broke" is:

  a  to be ill

  b  to be sad

  c  to be without money

  d  to be without friends

  e  to be in love

10 Which of these words means "hard-working"?

  a  flighty

  b  industrial

  c  job

  d  conscience

  e  industrious

11 What is this man holding?

  a  a dummy

  b  a doll

  c  a docker

  d  a toy

  e  a puppet

12 Which of the following is an example of crockery?

  a  a knife

  b  a car

  c  a cup

  d  a banana

  e  a frying pan

# 33 The sea-shore

Rearrange the letters to find out the names of the things in the following drawing:

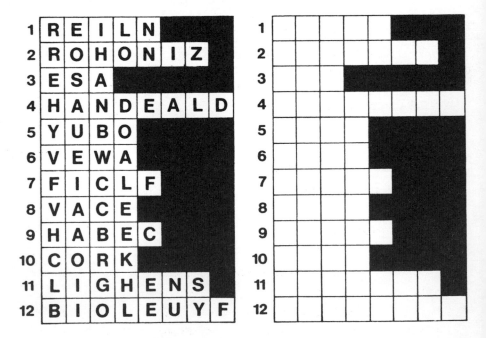

| | | | | | | |
|---|---|---|---|---|---|---|
| **1** | R | E | I | L | N | |
| **2** | R | O | H | O | N | I | Z |
| **3** | E | S | A | | | |
| **4** | H | A | N | D | E | A | L | D |
| **5** | Y | U | B | O | | |
| **6** | V | E | W | A | | |
| **7** | F | I | C | L | F | |
| **8** | V | A | C | E | | |
| **9** | H | A | B | E | C | |
| **10** | C | O | R | K | | |
| **11** | L | I | G | H | E | N | S |
| **12** | B | I | O | L | E | U | Y | F |

# 34 Prepositions 2

Fill in the missing prepositions in the following sentences.

1 I'm not very keen ................ classical music.
  a  of             b  on            c  for

2 He lives ................ the sea.
  a  on             b  at            c  near

3 For the last time – will you listen ................ me!
  a  to             b  on            c  at

4 I see that John's finally got engaged ................ Janina.
  a  with          b  by            c  to

5 There are too many exceptions ................ the rule in English.
  a  by            b  to            c  with

6 My brother's an authority ................ women.
  a  on             b  about       c  with

7 Did you receive that letter ................ Keith?
  a  by            b  off           c  from

8 His music was inspired ................ Beethoven.
  a  of             b  by            c  from

9 Everyone knows that women are equal ................ men.
  a  with          b  among      c  to

10 A lot of people were killed ................ the war.
  a  under       b  for           c  during

11 You're quite right. I agree ................ you completely.
  a  with          b  on            c  by

12 This is something my wife bought me ................ my birthday.
  a  to             b  for           c  at

13 Would you like milk or water ................ the meal?
  a  with          b  for           c  to

14 I stayed ................ a marvellous hotel last summer.
  a  on             b  by            c  at

15 ................ you and me, I think our teacher's stupid.
  a  with          b  between     c  among

# 35 Parts of a car

Match up the following words and numbers:

| | | | | | | |
|---|---|---|---|---|---|---|
| windscreen wipers | . . . . . | driving mirrors | . . . . . | tyre | . . . . . |
| headlight | . . . . . | bumper | . . . . . | seatbelt | . , . . . |
| windscreen | . . . . . | bonnet | . . . . . | indicator | . . . . . |
| radiator grill | . . . . . | boot | . . . . . | number plate | . . . . . |
| exhaust pipe | . . . . . | | | | |

| | | | | | | |
|---|---|---|---|---|---|---|
| steering wheel | . . . . . | hand brake | . . . . . | clutch | . . . . . |
| speedometer | . . . . . | petrol gauge | . . . . . | radio | . . . . . |
| foot brake | . . . . . | accelerator pedal | . . . . . | horn | . . . . . |
| glove compartment | . . . . . | gear stick | . . . . . | | |

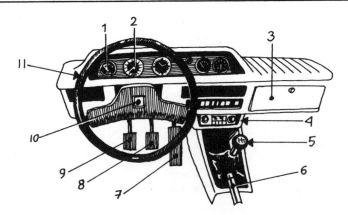

# 36 Add a letter

Add **one letter** to each of the following words (in any place) to form a new word. A clue is given to help you.

1 RAN    RAIN    can spoil a day at the seaside.

2 OAR    .......    the sound a lion makes

3 EAR    .......    a fruit

4 RULE    .......    you use one to draw straight lines

5 COD    .......    it is like this in winter

6 MEN    .......    the opposite of generous

7 RAM    .......    Americans call it a streetcar

8 HAVE    .......    something most men do every day

9 SAP    .......    keeps you clean

10 EASE    .......    artists use one to hold their canvas

11 RAVE    .......    it means you are not afraid

12 PEN    .......    pubs in England do this twice a day

13 ITCH    .......    "supernatural" woman

14 TROLL    .......    to walk

15 SORE    .......    American word for shop

16 SEAL    .......    it is against the law to do this

17 TALE    .......    the opposite of fresh (e.g. bread)

18 HARP    .......    the opposite of blunt

19 SEE    .......    to look for

20 WEAR    .......    very tired

21 TIN    .......    very small

22 ALE    .......    a story

23 LAME    .......    seen in a fire

24 FAT    .......    people once thought our Earth was this

25 HOSE    .......    an animal

# 37 Cartoons

In the following cartoons, the captions (i.e. the words that go with a cartoon) have got mixed up, so that each cartoon has been printed with the wrong caption under it. Work out the correct caption for each cartoon.

| Cartoon | | Correct caption | Cartoon | | Correct caption |
|---|---|---|---|---|---|
| 1 | – | ........ | 6 | – | ........ |
| 2 | – | ........ | 7 | – | ........ |
| 3 | – | ........ | 8 | – | ........ |
| 4 | – | ........ | 9 | – | ........ |
| 5 | – | ........ | 10 | – | ........ |

1  YOU ARE NOT STILL ANGRY AT ME, ARE YOU, DARLING?

2  DAD, THIS IS TOM, HE WORKS WITH COMPUTERS.

3  SAY CHEESE!

4  BUT WHAT MAKES YOU THINK YOU'VE BEEN WATCHING TOO MUCH TELEVISION, MRS GREY?

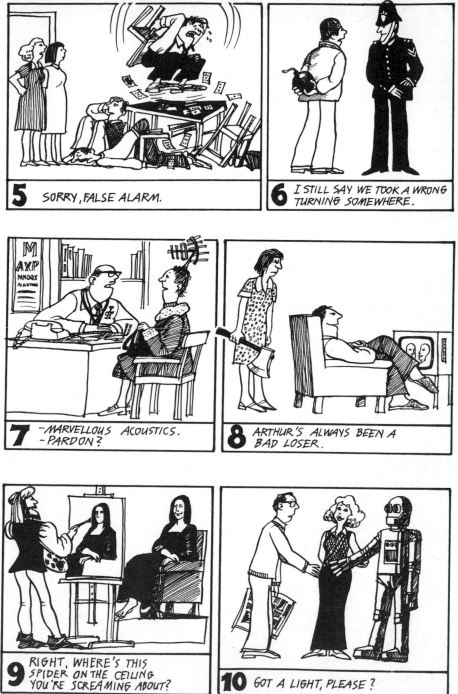

# 38 Too many words

Replace the words in bold type in following sentences with a single word. (The first letter of the world is given.)

1 The reason I like my present flat is that I have such friendly **people living next-door.** (n...............................)

2 The "Guinness Book of Records" is published **once every year.** (a....................)

3 After thinking about it for a long time, I finally **made up my mind** to take the job. (d...............................)

4 "I'm frightened", she **said in a very quiet voice.** (w...............................)

5 Last week I was **asked if I would like to go** to a birthday party. (i..........................)

6 My **sister's daughter** was taken to hospital last week. (n...............................)

7 At the end of the performance, the **people sitting in the theatre** applauded loudly. (a...............................)

8 I was totally **tired and worn out** after the football match on Saturday. (e...............................)

9 A ship could be seen on the **line where the sky seemed to meet the sea.** (h...............................)

10 I can't stand **people who pretend to be good but aren't really.** (h......................)

11 I want you to come here **without any delay whatsoever.** (i...............................)

12 I regret to inform you that you have **not managed to pass** the exam. (f...............)

# 39 British and American English

Fill in the British or American words in the following sentences. Give the British word for sentences 1–5 and the American one for sentences 6–10.

1 Now, madam, if you'd just open the ................,
   (hood)
   I'll check your battery for you.

2 It was a black car, Inspector, a Ford I think. But
   I'm afraid I didn't get a chance to see the ...............
   ................ (license
   plate)

3 One thing you should remember about England is
   that people always .................... when waiting for
   (stand in line)
   a bus.

4 Oh, Peter, I wonder if you could pop down to the
   .................... for me and get a bottle of whisky?
   (liquor store)

5 I'd like a .............. ticket to Hastings, please.
   (one-way)

6 The baby's crying, darling. I think he wants his
   ..............
   (dummy)

7 Go and .......................... before you have a meal,
   (wash your hands)
   there's a good boy.

8 There's something wrong with the hot water ..........
   ........................ It's running cold. (tap)

9 Excuse me, where's the nearest ........................
   (public con-
   ............. please?
   venience)

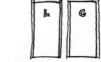

10 We could play a game of poker if someone has a
   ............................... of cards.
   (pack)

# 40 Puzzle it out 2 – Who's who at the party?

Read through the sentences below, then see if you can work out the names of the people at the party.

Mr Graham has fair hair.

Mr Collins is talking to Mrs Jones.

Mr Jones' wife is not wearing a striped dress.

Father Browne is a priest.

Mrs Collins is talking to Mr Gibson.

The man with Father Brown is married to the woman with dark hair.

Mr Gibson has his back to Mr Graham.

Mrs Collins has long, blonde hair.

The husband of the woman in the striped dress is smoking a pipe.

Number 1 is  . . . . . . . . . . . . . . . . . . . . . . .

Number 2 is  . . . . . . . . . . . . . . . . . . . . . . .

Number 3 is  . . . . . . . . . . . . . . . . . . . . . . .

Number 4 is  . . . . . . . . . . . . . . . . . . . . . . .

Number 5 is  . . . . . . . . . . . . . . . . . . . . . . .

Number 6 is  . . . . . . . . . . . . . . . . . . . . . . .

Number 7 is  . . . . . . . . . . . . . . . . . . . . . . .

Number 8 is  . . . . . . . . . . . . . . . . . . . . . . .

# 41 Confusing words

Choose the correct word in each of the following sentences.

1 You haven't (lent/borrowed) my rubber, have you, Paul?
2 He sat down (besides/beside) an old man with a white beard who looked and smelt as though he hadn't washed for weeks.
3 See that large (building/house) over there? Well, that's where I work. I've got an office on the sixth floor.
4 Was it (funny/fun) at the party on Friday?
5 The (nature/countryside) around this town is very flat and uninspiring.
6 The injured man was (laying/lying) on the road close to the wreckage of his car.
7 Who (taught/learnt) you to play the guitar, Fred?
8 Those of you who wish to come to the Zoo this afternoon, please (raise/rise) your hands.
9 When I heard that I'd been given the job I felt very (lucky/happy) indeed.
10 I usually (go up/get up) at 7.30 every morning.
11 Why don't you (take/bring) your girlfriend with you next time? We'd love to meet her.
12 Is it all right if I (go with/follow) you to the concert on Friday, Pam?
13 Sussex is my favourite (landscape/county) in England.
14 I didn't have time to (do/make) the beds this morning.
15 Amsterdam is a city full of (channels/canals).
16 I've been (sparing/saving) for years to buy a house.
17 Would you (check/control) these figures, Mr Brown – just to make sure they're correct?
18 It's a lot of (job/work) looking after children.
19 I prefer to (hire/rent) a television than buy one.
20 The answer to the crossword is on the (backside/back).
21 I thought you said you (were going to/should) give up smoking?
22 Our new neighbours invited me in for a cup of tea this morning. I must say they seem a very (nice/sympathetic) couple.
23 Was it Bell who (invented/discovered) the telephone?
24 I wonder if I might have a (recipe/receipt) for the things I've bought?
25 Oh, Jan, could you (remember/remind) me to phone the dentist this afternoon to make an appointment for Sally?

26 I wonder if you'd mind (bringing/fetching) John from next door? He's wanted on the telephone.
27 What (more/else) did you do in Spain, apart from swimming and sun-bathing?
28 I've just bought a record of Beethoven's Fifth symphony (conducted/directed) by Karajan.
29 When we moved into our new flat I had to sell my (grand/wing) piano because there wasn't enough room for it.
30 We'll have to change the curtains, darling. They don't (pass/match) the new suite. They're the wrong colour altogether.

# 42 Opposites – verbs

Find the opposites of the words on the left. Choose from the ones on the right.
Number 1 has been done for you.

1  to lend       to *borrow* ..................................
2  to vanish     to ..................................
3  to remember   to ..................................
4  to hurry      to ..................................
5  to detest     to ..................................
6  to insult     to ..................................
7  to sell       to ..................................
8  to depart     to ..................................
9  to increase   to ..................................
10 to attack     to ..................................
11 to encourage  to ..................................
12 to expand     to ..................................
13 to improve    to ..................................
14 to punish     to ..................................
15 to support    to ..................................

purchase /buy
decrease
defend
deteriorate /get
               worse
arrive
appear
take one's time
discourage
oppose
reward
forget
borrow
praise
adore
contract

# 43 Classifications

Write one name for each of the following groups. Before starting, look at the example.

1 Mercury, Mars, Venus, Saturn

2 apricot, date, grape, peach

3 Buddhism, Christianity, Judaism, Islam

4 cathedral, block of flats, museum, department store

5 Swiss, Dutch, Welsh, Belgian

6 golf, polo, rugby, wrestling

7 slowly, better, softly, enthusiastically

8 bow and arrow, dagger, machine gun, hand grenade

9 Gaelic, Hebrew, Yiddish, Swahili

10 leek, Brussels sprouts, turnip, spinach

11 mallet, plane, electric drill, screwdriver

12 pounds, kilos, grammes, ounces

13 corduroy, cotton, satin, crinoline

14 necklace, earrings, locket, bracelet

15 arrowroot, chicory, parsley, sage

16 smallpox, measles, mumps, bronchitis

17 minuet, tango, jive, polka

18 by, from, in, on

19 arson, theft, rape, fraud

20 250, 6, 27, 99

# 44 Types of transport

Write the number of each drawing next to the correct word or words.

| | |
|---|---|
| saloon car | . . . . . |
| caravan | . . . . . |
| van | . . . . . |
| hovercraft | . . . . . |
| submarine | . . . . . |
| estate car | . . . . . |
| articulated lorry | . . . . . |
| sports car | . . . . . |
| tanker | . . . . . |
| transporter | . . . . . |
| motorbike | . . . . . |
| yacht | . . . . . |
| coach | . . . . . |
| lorry | . . . . . |
| bus | . . . . . |
| barge | . . . . . |
| ambulance | . . . . . |
| taxi | . . . . . |
| canoe | . . . . . |
| tram | . . . . . |

# 45 Synonyms – more adjectives

Give a synonym for each of the words in brackets in the following sentences. Choose from the ones below. Number 1 has been done for you.

| | | | |
|---|---|---|---|
| giddy | hopeless | immature | amiable |
| chatty | absurd | reliable | famished |
| stingy | mad | disgraceful | conscious |
| intentional | pensive | weird | |

1 There's only one way of describing Hitler – he was completely (insane)
   _mad_ .................................

2 A good friend is someone who is kind, considerate and totally (dependable)
   ...............................................

3 Our new boss isn't too bad at all. In fact, she's quite (likeable) ........................
   .............. really.

4 You are (aware) ................................... of the fact that he's married, aren't
   you?

5 I wish you'd grow up! You're so (childish) ................................... !

6 I didn't mean to break it – it wasn't (deliberate) ...................................

7 That's the last time I go to a party with Simon! His behaviour last night was
   absolutely (disgusting) ...................................

8 I always get very (dizzy) ................................... when I stand on the top of
   high buildings.

9 What do you mean you can't afford to buy me a drink? Don't be so (mean)
   ...................................! You've got a lot more money than I have!

10 I could eat a horse! I'm (really hungry) ...................................!

11 Take those trousers off – you look (ridiculous) ................................... in
   them!

12 Our new neighbours are very (talkative) ..................................., aren't they?

13 You're looking rather (thoughtful) ................................... this morning,
   Jennifer. What's up?

14 6–1 we lost! 6–1! You played like a team of grannies! You were (pathetic)
   ...................................!

15 Charles has some really (peculiar) ................................... ideas sometimes,
   doesn't he?

# 46 From Bear to Coat

Change the word BEAR into COAT in eleven stages, changing only **one letter** at time.

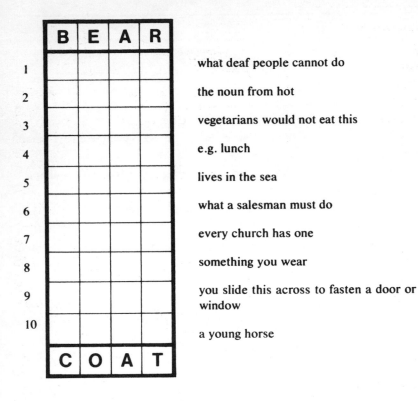

| | B | E | A | R | |
|---|---|---|---|---|---|
| 1 | | | | | what deaf people cannot do |
| 2 | | | | | the noun from hot |
| 3 | | | | | vegetarians would not eat this |
| 4 | | | | | e.g. lunch |
| 5 | | | | | lives in the sea |
| 6 | | | | | what a salesman must do |
| 7 | | | | | every church has one |
| 8 | | | | | something you wear |
| 9 | | | | | you slide this across to fasten a door or window |
| 10 | | | | | a young horse |
| | C | O | A | T | |

# 47 Bits and pieces 1

Write the number of each drawing next to the correct word.

| | |
|---|---|
| hot water bottle | . . . . . |
| dummy | . . . . . |
| handbag | . . . . . |
| hamper | . . . . . |
| nutcracker | . . . . . |
| clothes rack | . . . . . |
| hinge | . . . . . |
| thimble | . . . . . |
| curler | . . . . . |
| razor blade | . . . . . |
| tweezers | . . . . . |
| wallet | . . . . . |
| purse | . . . . . |
| rawlplug | . . . . . |
| jackplug | . . . . . |

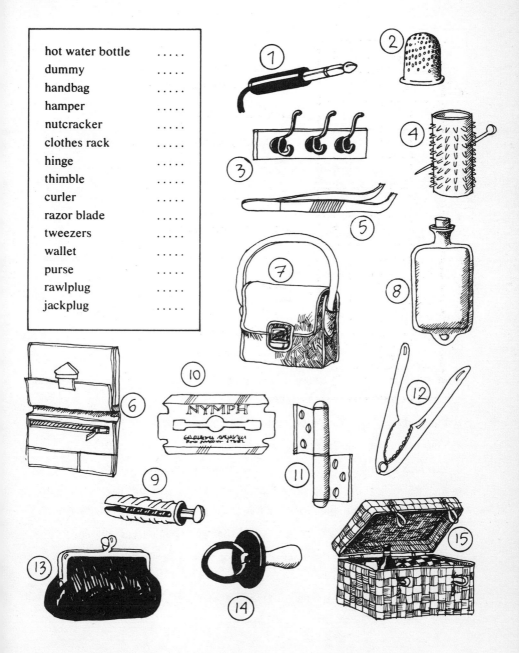

# 48 Missing words – books, etc.

Put the following words in the correct sentences.

| | | |
|---|---|---|
| encyclopedia | diary | album |
| manual | catalogue | register |
| newspaper | log | calendar |
| dictionary | cookery book | time-table |
| directory | map | atlas |
| index | library | brochure |

1 You read a ..................................... to find out what has happened recently, both in your own country and in the rest of the world.

2 A ..................................... is a book or booklet which gives you a list of goods or books for sale, plus their prices.

3 An ..................................... helps you to find the position of a place or a country anywhere in the world.

4 If you can't afford to buy books, then you can always borrow them from the .....................................

5 An ..................................... is a book (or a set of books) dealing with every branch of knowledge in alphabetical order.

6 You can keep a collection of photographs or autographs in an ..........................

7 You record personal events and happenings in a .....................................

8 You look at a ..................................... to know the date and the month.

9 An ..................................... is an alphabetical list at the back of a book of names, subjects, etc. mentioned in it and the pages where they can be found.

10 If you have a ..................................... then you shouldn't get lost.

11 If you want to find out the times of trains or buses you should consult a ..............
.....................

12 When something goes wrong with your car, you can always try to repair it yourself with the help of a car.....................................

13 If you don't know where to go on holiday, why don't you get a holiday .............. ...................... from your nearest Travel Agency?

14 If you don't know a person's telephone number, you can always look it up in the telephone ....................................

15 If you want to find out how to make a particular dish you can look in a .............. ......................

16 You use a .................................... to find out the meaning of a word.

17 The captain of a ship fills in a .................................... every day.

18 You look at a .................................... if you want to find out how often some- one has attended school or a course.

# 49 Word association 2

Underline two of the words on the right which are associated with or are part of the word on the left. Number 1 has been done for you.

1 BABY      inspire, <u>cot</u>, <u>dummy</u>, creeping, barn

2 DENTIST      meat, toothache, skirt, denture, bore

3 LAW COURT      sentence, dumb, judge, wall, sing

4 SEWING      pattern, stick, tug, stitch, saxophone

5 TRAIN      lucky, compartment, spare, luggage-rack, trap

6 OFFICE      stable, mincer, gem, filing-cabinet, typist

7 PHOTOGRAPH      duck, slides, snapshot, ruler, whisper

8 SEASIDE      bath, stranded, beach, cough, deckchair

9 FUNERAL      coffee, widow, bride, duster, cemetery

10 BIRD      pigeon, trunk, beak, nib, foxglove

11 TENNIS      like, net, offside, umpire, Wembley

12 JACKET      wear, rusty, lapel, smile, crooked

13 RIVER      fly, bank, mining, Danube, cellar

14 NEWSPAPER      circulation, backside, lettuce, editor, reduction

15 BED      headboard, ponytail, slim, blanket, madness

16 CAR      slip, tired, bonnet, deck, radiator

17 CAT      purr, swan, bark, paw, river

18 HOUSE      sob, landing, wind, mortgage, tenor

19 CARDS      joking, clubs, dark, clover, shuffle

20 CHURCH      alter, prayer, hymn, audience, staffroom

# 50 Bits and pieces 2

Write the number of each drawing next to the correct word.

locket ..... 

alarm clock ..... 

stamp ..... 

kitchen timer ..... 

file ..... 

egg timer ..... 

flippers ..... 

pencil ..... 

lipstick ..... 

compact ..... 

cotton reel ..... 

headphones ..... 

identification disc ..... 

decanter ..... 

sunglasses ..... 

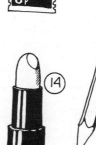

# 51 Missing words – adverbs

Put the following adverbs in the correct sentences. Use each word once only.

| | | | |
|---|---|---|---|
| absolutely | comfortably | extremely | normally |
| angrily | completely | finally | patiently |
| annually | continuously | fortunately | seriously |
| anxiously | courageously | happily | soundly |
| briefly | deliberately | heavily | unexpectedly |
| carefully | easily | lately | violently |

1 They say it's difficult to get a job nowadays, but I found one ....................

2 You'd better take an umbrella with you. It's raining ................... at the moment.

3 It's been a really hard day today, so I should sleep ................... tonight.

4 Living very close to the motorway, cars and lorries ................... passed their house during the night. It was really hard to sleep sometimes.

5 'Mind your own business!' he snapped ....................

6 The trapped animal struggled ................... to free itself.

7 It was no accident! She did it ...................! I saw her.

8 David only had time to explain ................... what had happened at the meeting because he was in a hurry.

9 I ................... have toast and tea for breakfast but today for a change I had a boiled egg.

10 Have you seen Pam and Dave's new house? It's ................... enormous!

11 My grandfather was sitting so ................... in my new armchair that he fell fast asleep.

12 The crowd waited ................... for the Queen to arrive at the theatre.

13 When he returned home to his village after more than thirty years, he found to his disappointment that everything had ..................... changed – not only the buildings and the people, but even the way of life.

14 My parents arrived at my flat .....................; I had no idea they were even in London.

15 There was an accident on the motorway this morning, but ..................... no one was ..................... injured.

16 The soldiers fought ..................... but in the end were forced to surrender.

17 My wife and I have been ..................... married for eighteen years.

18 The *Guinness Book of Records* is published .....................

19 The weather has been ..................... cold recently. In fact, this is the coldest November for over seventy-five years.

20 Any idea what's happened to Annie? I haven't seen much of her .....................

21 At his seventh attempt he ..................... managed to pass his driving test.

22 The mother waited ..................... by the phone for news of her missing daughter.

23 The roads are very icy tonight, so drive .....................

# 52 Anagrams

Sort out the following anagrams. To help you, the first letter of the answer is given. Before starting, look at the example.

Change **thorn** into a direction.     n. *orth*

1 Change **admirer** into the opposite of single.     m................

2 Change **alloy** into what a good friend should be.     l................

3 Change **aloft** into the opposite of sink.     f................

4 Change **backward** into another word for disadvantage.     d................

5 Change **blame** into a way of walking.     a................

6 Change **bristle** into something you sometimes get when you have new shoes.     b................

7 Change **danger** into something most houses have.     g................

8 Change **disk** into what can happen to a car when the roads are icy.     s................

9 Change **each** into a word to do with pain.     a................

10 Change **fade** into a word that means you can't hear.     d................

11 Change **false** into small insects cats and dogs sometimes have in their fur. (*plural*)     f................

12 Change **general** into a word that means make bigger.     e................

13 Change **impart** into a part of the body.     a................

14 Change **insures** into a time of day.     s................

15 Change **later** into another word for change.     a................

16 Change **master** into a small river.     s................

17 Change **ocean** into a type of water transport.     c................

18 Change **react** into a container, e.g. for beer, milk, etc.     c................

19 Change **skis** into a sign of affection. k................

20 Change **teach** into a word to do with dishonesty. c................

21 Change **miles** into a sign of happiness. s................

22 Change **palm** into something found in the living room. l................

23 Change **solemn** into a type of fruit. (*plural*) m................

24 Change **mope** into something you can read and enjoy. p................

25 Change **dances** into a word that means to go up. a................

26 Change **inch** into a part of the face. c................

27 Change **ulcer** into the opposite of kind. c................

28 Change **drawer** into a word to do with money. r................

29 Change **live** into another word for wicked. e................

30 Change **tutor** into a type of fish (usually found in rivers). t................

# 53 What's the verb?

Complete the following sentences with a suitable verb. Choose from the following. Use each verb once only. Number 1 has been done for you.

| | | | | |
|---|---|---|---|---|
| break | cross | hang | play | tie |
| build | deliver | learn | read | wash |
| catch | drive | listen to | ride | watch |
| celebrate | feed | lose | run | wear |
| change | fly | open | sign | win |
| cook | grow | paint | tell | write |

1 Breakfast, lunch and dinner are things you ...*cook*......

2 Dishes, your hair, the car are things you ....................

3 Your name, essays, letters are things you ....................

4 Jewellery, shoes, glasses are things you ....................

5 The radio, music, advice are things you ....................

6 Roses, plants, your hair are things you ....................

7 Houses, bridges, buildings are things you ....................

8 Newspapers, novels, someone's palm are things you ....................

9 Trains, buses, a cold are things you ....................

10 Letters, babies, parcels are things you ....................

11 Television, films, football matches are things you ....................

12 Babies, pets, starving people are things you ....................

13 The piano, cards, tennis are things you ....................

14 Planes, spaceships, kites are things you ....................

15 Foreign languages, using a computer, a lesson are things you ....................

16 Pictures, your nails, walls are things you .....................

17 Doors, windows, a bank account are things you .....................

18 Shoelaces, knots, ribbons are things you .....................

19 Cars, buses, lorries are things you .....................

20 Washing, pictures, wallpaper are things you .....................

21 A contract, cheques, your name are things you .....................

22 Money, your mind, jobs are things you .....................

23 A border, a room, a road are things you .....................

24 Christmas, your birthday, victories are things you .....................

25 A promise, your leg, a window are things you .....................

26 Lies, stories, jokes are things you .....................

27 A company, a race, English courses are things you .....................

28 Your job, your memory, weight are things you .....................

29 Bicycles, horses, motorbikes are things you .....................

30 Competitions, prizes, battles are things you .....................

# 54 Choose the word 3

Underline one word in each of the three pairs of brackets to make the most logical sentence. Before starting, look at the example.

The (<u>teacher</u>, mechanic, solicitor) wrote the (letter, <u>answer</u>, notebook) on the (floor, <u>board</u>, ceiling).

1 The (referee, soldier, caretaker) blew his (ballroom, whistle, candle) to end the (match, battle, lesson).

2 Sally (phoned, decided, cycled) to have a (check-up, wedding, party) on her (weekend, birthday, flat).

3 The (bird, dog, cow) was (grazing, sitting, swimming) on the (pavement, nest, lamp-post).

4 The (cooker, man, sheep) put his (bicycle, comb, brother) in his (floor, drawer, pocket).

5 James (borrowed, caught, made) six (teeth, eggs, books) from the (library, station, post office).

6 We bought a new (sofa, shower, lawn) for the (kitchen, living-room, garden) in the January (moth, sales, shop).

7 The (artist, shop assistant, chef) placed the (motorbike, casserole, guitar) in the (drawer, garage, oven).

8 That (man, shop, woman) drove her (car, flat, father) into a (carpet, tree, circus).

9 The (plane, boat, train) now standing at (station, platform, lane) seven has just arrived (to, for, from) Brighton.

10 After listening to the (weather forecast, CD, wind) they decided to (try on, cancel, post) their (order, newspaper, picnic).

11 The (opera, blackbird, choir) sang a (song, music, performance) at the Christmas (shopping, concert, Eve).

12 The (planets, groups, flowers) Mars and Jupiter are clearly (marked, visible, placed) in the (east, clear, night) sky.

13 On (one o'clock, Thursday, June) we went to the (shops, airport, beach) for a (swim, meal, haircut).

14 The (coffee, snow, water) began to (freeze, boil, melt) in the (sunshine, day, saucepan).

15 The (students, father, pigeons) were waiting anxiously for the (shape, results, arrival) of their (tickets, neighbour, exams).

16 All (those, who, after) wishing to go to the concert please (rise, raise, lift) your (hands, voices, level).

17 The (doctor, teacher, policeman) put his (ruler, baton, stethoscope) to the patient's (house, chest, pockets).

18 His (manners, handwriting, speech) was (terrible, marvellous, backwards). I just couldn't (respect, eat, read) it.

19 A British (car, passport, flag) is (valid, remembered, worn) in most foreign (countries, languages, stamps).

20 The (pedestrian crossing, car, computer) is a wonderful (invention, discovery, hobby) which has greatly increased (conversation, productivity, collection).

# 55 Right or wrong?

Is the word in **bold** type in each of the following sentences used correctly or not? If you think it is, put a tick (✓) in the RIGHT column. If you think it isn't, put a tick in the WRONG column. (You can also try to explain why it is used wrongly.)

|  | RIGHT | WRONG |
|---|---|---|
| 1 These shoes don't **fit** me – they're the wrong colour. | .......... | .......... |
| 2 You would probably feel very flattered if someone told you that you were **conceited**. | .......... | .......... |
| 3 He makes us laugh a lot. He's very **witty**. | .......... | .......... |
| 4 The person in charge of a museum is called the **curator**. | .......... | .......... |
| 5 He watched the horse-race through **binoculars**. | .......... | .......... |
| 6 You have to do it – it's **compulsory**. | .......... | .......... |
| 7 I never had very much money as a student, so I used to **hijack** a lot. | .......... | .......... |
| 8 A **timid** person is usually very brave. | .......... | .......... |
| 9 You would probably feel very **embarrassed** if your trousers fell down in public. | .......... | .......... |
| 10 People who ride motorbikes should wear **crash-helmets**. | .......... | .......... |
| 11 If you save money in a bank, you usually get **interest** on it. | .......... | .......... |
| 12 A synonym for stubborn is **mean**. | .......... | .......... |
| 13 I'm looking for the **maternity ward**. My wife's expecting a baby. | .......... | .......... |
| 14 In Britain you usually wear a **vest** under a shirt, not over it. | .......... | .......... |

15 I know him well – he's an **acquaintance** of mine.  .......... ..........

16 A **torch** will help you to see in the dark.  .......... ..........

17 Most people like having **sunstroke** in the summer.  .......... ..........

18 You wear a **beret** on your head.  .......... ..........

19 **Prunes** are my favourite vegetables.  .......... ..........

20 **Trunk, twig** and **willow** are all words connected
with a tree.  .......... ..........

21 He must have run all the way – he's **panting**.  .......... ..........

22 Most gardeners would be proud of their **weeds**.  .......... ..........

23 A policeman usually carries a **truncheon** for
defence.  .......... ..........

24 I'm very **supernatural**. I think it's very unlucky
to walk under ladders, for example.  .......... ..........

25 It's very hot. Let's sit in the **shadow**.  .......... ..........

# 56 Choose the adjective

Complete the sentences below with an adjective that is similar in meaning to the word in **bold** type. Choose from the words on the right.

| | | |
|---|---|---|
| 1 A **wealthy** person is | ............................................. | clumsy |
| 2 An **abrupt** ending is | ............................................. | dependable |
| 3 An **inquisitive** person is | ............................................. | fair |
| 4 An **awkward** person is | ............................................. | fast |
| 5 An **idle** person is | ............................................. | faulty |
| 6 A **contented** person is | ............................................. | lazy |
| 7 **Raw** fish is | ............................................. | lucky |
| 8 An **ancient** monument is | ............................................. | polite |
| 9 A **fortunate** escape is | ............................................. | priceless |
| 10 A **brisk** pace is | ............................................. | rich |
| 11 A **drowsy** person is | ............................................. | ridiculous |
| 12 A **conceited** person is | ............................................. | satisfied |
| 13 A **reliable** person is | ............................................. | sleepy |
| 14 An **invaluable** possession is | ............................................. | slight |
| 15 A **slender** chance is | ............................................. | sudden |
| 16 An **unbiased** report is | ............................................. | tasty |
| 17 A **delicious** meal is | ............................................. | uncooked |
| 18 A **courteous** person is | ............................................. | vain |
| 19 A **defective** article is | ............................................. | very curious |
| 20 An **absurd** idea is | ............................................. | very old |

# 57 What's the rhyming word?

Fill in the missing words in the following sentences by choosing a word which rhymes with the word in **bold** type at the end of each sentence. Before starting, look at the example.

I'll m......*ee*......t you on Friday at 7.30. **heat**

1 We can't eat this bread, it's s.....................e. **rail**
2 Shall I p.....................r the tea or will you? **four**
3 Please don't t.....................e your brother. He doesn't like it. **please**
4 We've just bought a new s.....................e of furniture for the living-room. **feet**
5 The Arsenal defender was sent off for f.....................l play half-way through the second half. **howl**
6 My brother has played on the Centre C.....................t at Wimbledon. He's a really good tennis player. **port**
7 The ambulance soon arrived at the s.....................e of the crime. **mean**
8 It's getting very late. I d.....................t if they'll come now. **out**
9 My wife collects a.....................e furniture. **leek**
10 'This is none of your business, Jane, so please don't i.....................e!' Samantha said angrily to her sister. **deer**
11 We stayed at a very p.....................e village in the Swiss Alps. **desk**
12 After rising for many years, the number of people buying new cars is once again starting to d.....................e. **wine**
13 The government's anti-smoking c.....................n has only achieved moderate success. **rain**
14 Keep the r.....................t in case you need to change the goods. **meat**
15 The fox was caught in a s.....................e and couldn't escape. **chair**
16 We will need to s.....................y the land before we start building any houses on it. **play**
17 I can't come with you tonight. I've got to r.....................e the school play. **purse**
18 They had a big party to c.....................e passing their exams. **wait**
19 There was a large brown s.....................n on the carpet where he had spilled the coffee. **lane**
20 There was a huge c.....................r from the waiting crowd as the queen arrived at the theatre. **fear**
21 My brother has a y.....................t and regularly sails to France in it. **hot**
22 You'd better not speak to Samantha today. She's in a really bad m.....................d. **rude**

# 58 Same word – different meaning

Some words in English can have more than one meaning. Read through the pairs of sentences below and try to work out what the missing words are. Number 1 has been done for you.

1  *watch*  How often do you ........ television?

Her parents promised to buy her a ........ as soon as she had learnt to tell the time.

2  ...................  They got their water from a ........ at the bottom of the garden.

She was ill but she's ........ again now.

3  ...................  We hopped over the ........ into our neighbour's garden.

A lot of actors have to learn to ........ and ride a horse – especially for parts in films like *The Three Musketeers*.

4  ...................  Let's go out tonight for a ........, I'm fed up of cooking.

Have you got any ........, Pam? I've only got a £10 note on me.

5  ...................  My brother can't stand the sight of blood. It always makes him .........

Her voice on the phone was so ........ that I could hardly hear it.

6  ...................  This ........ account offers 5.5% interest.

He sat on the river ........ to fish.

7  ...................  He wants to get married, but he can't ........ the thought of leaving his mother.

We saw a dancing ......... when we were on holiday in Russia last summer.

8  ...................  This music's got a very good .........

Argentina ......... Germany 2–0 in the final.

9  ...................  He was knocked out by a sharp ........ to the head.

I volunteered to ....... up all the balloons for the children's party.

10  ...................  It's an informal party, so you don't need to wear a collar and ......... . You can go in jeans and a t-shirt.

She bent down to ........ up her shoelace.

11  ...................  The ........ of her nose was red.

The waitress was so friendly that he gave her a big .........

12 ..................... The terrorists tried to blow up the ........

One of the world's most popular card games is .........

13 ..................... A ........ had built its nest under our roof.

When she had a sore throat, she found it very difficult to ......... food.

14 ..................... There will be a ........ election at the end of next year.

The ........ ordered his troops to attack the village.

15 ..................... Use a first-class ........ if you want the letter to arrive by tomorrow.

Everyone began to ........ their feet in time to the music.

16 ..................... He bought a kilo of ........ coffee.

The ........ was covered with snow.

17 ..................... There was a drawing pin stuck in the ........ of his shoe.

You like fish, don't you? What does ........ taste like?

18 ..................... In Singapore, it is against the law to chew ........ in public.

His ........ began to bleed as he was brushing his teeth.

19 ..................... Autumn is my favourite .........

You should always remember to ........ food.

20 ..................... I'm tired. I think I'll go and ........ down for a while.

I didn't say that! That's a ........!

21 ..................... I need to go to the gym every day to try to get into ........ again.

A rugby ball has a different ........ to a football.

22 ..................... There were seven puppies altogether in the .........

People who have picnics should always remember to take their ........ home with them.

23 ..................... They found an unexploded ........ on the beach.

Don't forget to take the ........ off the egg before you eat it.

24 ..................... I'm looking for curtains that will ........ my carpet.

It was probably the most exciting football ........ they had ever seen.

25 ..................... I can't draw a straight line without using a .........

The ........ of this country used to be a king, but now it's a president.

# 59 Words with silent letters

Complete the crossword. Each word contains a silent letter (see example). If you need extra help, the first and last letters of each word are given at the bottom of the opposite page.

**Across**

1 One of the joints on your arm.

3 A large fish with pink flesh that lives in the sea but swims up rivers to lay its eggs. A popular dish at restaurants.

6 A ship that has sunk.

8 A visitor to your home.

10 Found in the kitchen. You often put cups, glasses, etc. inside it.

13 An imaginary creature. (There are lots of these in British gardens!)

14 A very large mammal that lives in the sea.

15 A chess piece. Also a type of soldier a long time ago who used to wear armour and fight on horseback.

17 A herb used in cooking.

19 To make things to wear (usually of wool). You normally use two needles.

20 Part of the leg.

21 A young cow.

23 To write your name, e.g. on a cheque or a document.

25 Found on the hand.

28 An explosive device.

29 What most people hope the sea will be when they travel.

30 What you do with your ears.

31 Permanently unable to speak.

**Down**

2 A fruit – often used in jam.

4 One of the seasons.

5 Unable to feel anything, e.g. as a result of being very cold.

7 The joint in your finger.

8 A small flying insect that bites.

9 A smell or perfume.

11 Money owed.

12 A type of tree. Also part of your hand.

14 What most people get with age – especially on the face.

15 An item of cutlery.
16 Someone who inherits.
18 Another word for truthful.
19 To tie together two pieces of rope, string, etc.
21 Something you use that is connected with hair.
22 Not obvious.
24 The spirit of a dead person.
26 Fifty percent of something.
27 Not correct.
30 A young sheep.

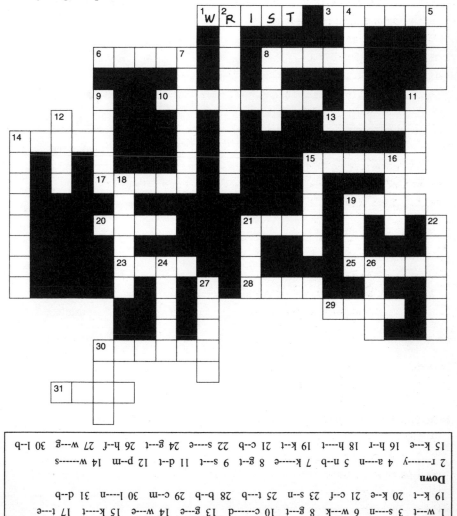

**Across**
1 w--t  3 s---n  6 w--k  8 g---t  10 c------d  13 g--e  14 w--e-e  15 k---l  17 t--e
19 k--t  20 k--e  21 c--f  23 s--n  25 t---b  28 b--b  29 c--m  30 l-----t  31 d--b

**Down**
2 r-------y  4 a----n  5 n--b  7 k-----e  8 g--t  9 s---t  11 d--t  12 p--m  14 w------s
15 k--e  16 h--r  18 h----t  19 k---t  21 c--b  22 s----e  24 g--t  26 h--f  27 w---g  30 l--b

# 60 Adjective + noun combinations

Complete the phrases on the left with the most suitable adjective. Choose from the words on the right. Use each adjective once only.

| | |
|---|---|
| 1 a .................... orange, pear | angry |
| 2 a .................... snake | bronze |
| 3 a .................... hill | bumpy |
| 4 a .................... meal | damp |
| 5 an .................... mob | deep |
| 6 a .................... friend, servant | delicious |
| 7 a .................... knife | fair |
| 8 an .................... message | haunted |
| 9 a .................... well, cut | infectious |
| 10 a .................... house | juicy |
| 11 a .................... injury | loyal |
| 12 .................... bread (*you can't eat it*) | lucky |
| 13 a .................... cloth | painful |
| 14 an .................... disease | parallel |
| 15 a .................... escape | poisonous |
| 16 a .................... sea | sharp |
| 17 .................... lines | stale |
| 18 a .................... complexion | steep |
| 19 a .................... road | stormy |
| 20 a .................... statue | urgent |

# Answers

## TEST 1

| | |
|---|---|
| coat hanger | 12 |
| potato peeler | 6 |
| lightbulb | 2 |
| colander | 7 |
| broom | 3 |
| plate | 4 |
| egg slicer | 9 |
| dustpan | 8 |
| carpet beater | 5 |
| scrubbing brush | 10 |
| cheese slicer | 11 |
| tea towel | 1 |

## TEST 2

1. attractive
2. enjoyable
3. big-headed
4. appalling
5. odd
6. enormous
7. obstinate
8. bashful
9. keen
10. authentic
11. cheeky
12. ample
13. unbelievable
14. vital
15. hilarious

## TEST 3

1. house
2. palace
3. monastery
4. convent
5. barracks
6. cell
7. caravan
8. igloo
9. hive
10. nest
11. kennel
12. stable
13. sty
14. web
15. eyrie

## TEST 4

Right order:
3 – 8 – 4 – 6 – 1 – 10 – 5 – 9 – 2 – 7

## TEST 5

| | |
|---|---|
| pepper mill | 6 |
| liquidizer/blender | 12 |
| fire guard | 11 |
| bowl | 10 |
| tray | 7 |
| briefcase | 2 |
| lemon squeezer | 4 |
| tea strainer | 9 |
| bellows | 5 |
| bottle opener | 3 |
| suitcase | 8 |
| ladle | 1 |

## TEST 6

1. harmful
2. mean
3. temporary
4. lazy
5. minute
6. hostile
7. exciting
8. timid
9. cheap
10. broad-minded
11. imaginary
12. wonderful
13. sudden
14. uninterested
15. unfortunate

## TEST 7

**Down**

1. Arab
2. India
3. Belgian
4. Czech
5. Canada
6. Swiss
7. Pole
8. Dane
9. Turkey
10. Vietnamese
11. Egypt
12. Swede

**Across**

1. Finn
2. New Zealand
3. Holland
4. Scotland
5. Australia
6. Greek
7. Jew
8. Peru
9. Norway
10. Eskimo
11. United States

## TEST 8

a ball of string
a bunch of grapes
an ear of corn
a cube of sugar
a pack of cards
a crate of beer
a pad of writing paper
a bar of chocolate
a punnet of strawberries
a string of beads
a bouquet of flowers
a quiver of arrows

## TEST 9

| | |
|---|---|
| chopping board | 8 |
| aerial | 4 |
| banister | 11 |
| curtains | 1 |
| door handle | 12 |
| doorbell | 7 |
| coffee filter | 5 |
| pillow | 10 |
| dustbin | 9 |
| umbrella | 2 |
| spatula | 6 |
| cushion | 3 |

## TEST 10

1  (c)
2  (a)
3  (c)
4  (c)
5  (d)
6  (b)
7  (b)
8  (c)
9  (a)
10  (d)
11  (b)
12  (a)

## TEST 11

Miss Rees is a cashier
Mr Berry is a caddie
Mr Guard is a caretaker
Miss Knowles is a solicitor
Mr Train is a porter
Mrs Plod is a postwoman
Mrs Carter is a surgeon
Mr Austin is a chauffeur
Mr Field is a farmer
Miss Sayer is a speech therapist

## TEST 12

1  ward
2  kitchen
3  cellar
4  attic
5  cabins
6  study
7  crypt
8  hold
9  larder
10  parlour
11  studio
12  lounge
13  dormitory

## TEST 13

| | |
|---|---|
| plane | 4 |
| file | 6 |
| axe | 12 |
| pliers | 1 |
| extension cable | 5 |
| jack | 8 |
| secateurs | 9 |
| watering can | 10 |
| sickle | 3 |
| vice | 7 |
| fire extinguisher | 11 |
| chisel | 2 |

## TEST 14

1  enter
2  vanished
3  purchased
4  detests
5  tripped
6  accomplish
7  altered
8  recollect
9  put off
10  scare
11  spoilt
12  moaning
13  occurred
14  inform
15  bragging

## TEST 15

Building number 1 is a church

Building number 2 is an Estate Agent's

Building number 3 is a museum

Building number 4 is an Art Gallery

Building number 5 is a betting shop (Turf accountant's)

Building number 6 is a cinema

Building number 7 is an undertaker's

Building number 8 is an office block

Building number 9 is the Town Hall

Building number 10 is a prison

## TEST 16

1  car
2  football
3  orchestra
4  flower
5  dog
6  wedding
7  house
8  guitar
9  bed
10  astronomy
11  soldier
12  radio
13  typewriter
14  pub
15  tennis
16  meal
17  river
18  shoe
19  hospital
20  music

## TEST 17

| | |
|---|---|
| stove (cooker) | 2 |
| washing machine | 4 |
| fridge | 10 |
| coffee table | 11 |
| bedside table | 6 |
| shower | 9 |
| bath | 3 |

| | | | |
|---|---|---|---|
| wardrobe | 5 | | |
| broom cupboard | 8 | | |
| fluorescent light | 7 | | |
| oil lamp | 12 | | |
| ceiling light | 1 | | |

**TEST 18**

1  big-headed
2  immature
3  intelligent
4  moody
5  sympathetic
6  rude
7  ambitious
8  eccentric
9  obstinate
10  strict

**TEST 19**

**Across**

1  orienteering
2  sailing
3  knitting
4  archaeology
5  bridge
6  gardening
7  weaving
8  camping
9  painting
10  table tennis
11  music
12  yoga

**Down**

1  photography
2  embroidery
3  gliding
4  stamp collecting
5  cycling
6  chess
7  cooking/cookery
8  dancing
9  riding
10  swimming
11  acting
12  ice skating
13  mah-jong
14  billiards

15  fishing
16  pottery

**TEST 20**

1  (b)
2  (a)
3  (c)
4  (b)
5  (c)
6  (a)
7  (c)
8  (c)
9  (a)
10  (b)
11  (b)
12  (b)
13  (c)
14  (c)
15  (a)

**TEST 21**

| | |
|---|---|
| shaving socket | 7 |
| record storage unit | 5 |
| time switch | 9 |
| window sill | 11 |
| fan heater | 1 |
| trolley | 2 |
| room divider | 12 |
| door knob | 8 |
| extractor fan | 3 |
| curtain rail | 10 |
| coat stand | 6 |
| window box | 4 |

**TEST 22**

Bill is Susan's father
Ted is Susan's brother
Ann is Susan's sister
Freda is Susan's cousin
Olive is Susan's aunt
Paul is Susan's brother-in-law

**TEST 23**

a pig grunts
a dog barks

a mouse squeaks
a cock crows
a frog croaks
an elephant trumpets
a hourse neighs
a lamb bleats
a lion roars
a cow lows

**TEST 24**

1  throat
2  Saturn
3  wallet
4  rabbit
5  saucer
6  spider
7  willow
8  salmon
9  vanish
10  blouse
11  skiing
12  eighty
13  pigeon
14  lawyer
15  guitar
16  nephew
17  lizard
18  radish
19  petrol
20  gutter

**TEST 25**

| | | |
|---|---|---|
| 1 | rugs | drugs |
| 2 | crows | crowds |
| 3 | wife | wire |
| 4 | daring | darling |
| 5 | heard | head |
| 6 | bust | but |
| 7 | God | Good |
| 8 | property | properly |
| 9 | polite | police |
| 10 | burning | turning |

**TEST 26**

| | |
|---|---|
| bow tie | 9 |
| bowler hat | 4 |
| beret | 5 |

cardigan 7
sweater 3
apron 2
gloves 1
braces 10
clogs 6
shorts 11
sandals 12
string vest 8

## TEST 27

1 (b)
2 (b)
3 (d)
4 (d)
5 (a)
6 (b)
7 (d)
8 (b)
9 (b)
10 (c)
11 (a)
12 (b)

## TEST 28

1 d
2 i
3 g
4 k
5 a
6 j
7 e
8 l
9 b
10 f
11 h
12 c

## TEST 29

Order of dialogue part:
– Oh, sorry!
– John! This is a surprise!
– Oh, I live here now.
– Yes. that's right. Sweden.
– About a month ago.
– No, only me.
– Well, as a matter of fact, we've decided to get a divorce.
– Ah well, it can't be helped. And there aren't any children fortunately.
– But anyway, enough of me. What are you doing these days?
– St. Richard's Comprehensive?
– You must enjoy it then.
– (Laughing) I see. Same old John. You haven't changed a bit.

## TEST 30

dartboard 6
tennis racquet 3
badminton racquet 8
air pistol 4
golf club 12
tent 2
chess set 11
dice 10
figure skate 13
ski stick 1
shin pad 14
dumbbell 9
shuttlecock 15
binoculars 5
ice hockey stick 7

## TEST 31

### 1 In a school

blackboard
desks
playground
pupils
staffroom

### 2 In the kitchen

cutlery
dishwasher
fridge
frying pan
sink unit

### 3 On a boat

crew
deck
funnel
portholes
rails

### 4 In a church

aisle
altar
congregation
pulpit
pew

### 5 On a jacket

button
collar
lapel
pocket
sleeve

### 6 In a hospital

matron
operating theatre
patients
stethoscope
ward

### 7 In an office

date stamp
filing cabinet
secretary
stapler
typewriter

### 8 On a car

boot
bumper
clutch
horn
seatbelt

## TEST 32

1 (c)
2 (c)
3 (c)
4 (c)

5 (b)
6 (e)
7 (d)
8 (a)
9 (c)
10 (e)
11 (a)
12 (c)

## TEST 33

1 liner
2 horizon
3 sea
4 headland
5 buoy
6 wave
7 cliff
8 cave
9 beach
10 rock
11 shingle
12 lifebuoy

## TEST 34

1 (b)
2 (c)
3 (a)
4 (c)
5 (b)
6 (a)
7 (c)
8 (b)
9 (c)
10 (c)
11 (a)
12 (b)
13 (a)
14 (c)
15 (b)

## TEST 35

| | |
|---|---|
| windscreen wipers | 3 |
| headlight | 12 |
| windscreen | 4 |
| radiator grill | 1 |
| exhaust pipe | 9 |
| driving mirrors | 5 |

| | |
|---|---|
| bumper | 8 |
| bonnet | 2 |
| boot | 7 |
| tyre | 10 |
| seatbelt | 6 |
| indicator | 11 |
| number plate | 13 |
| steering wheel | 11 |
| speedometer | 2 |
| foot brake | 8 |
| glove compartment | 3 |
| hand brake | 6 |
| petrol gauge | 1 |
| accelerator pedal | 7 |
| gear stick | 5 |
| clutch | 9 |
| radio | 4 |
| horn | 10 |

## TEST 36

1 rain
2 roar
3 pear
4 ruler
5 cold
6 mean
7 tram
8 shave
9 soap
10 easel
11 brave
12 open
13 witch
14 stroll
15 store
16 steal
17 stale
18 sharp
19 seek
20 weary
21 tiny
22 tale
23 flame
24 flat
25 horse

## TEST 37

1 – 5
2 – 6
3 – 9
4 – 7
5 – 8
6 – 10
7 – 4
8 – 1
9 – 3
10 – 2

## TEST 38

1 neighbours
2 annually
3 decided
4 whispered
5 invited
6 niece
7 audience
8 exhausted
9 horizon
10 hypocrites
11 immediately
12 failed

## TEST 39

1 bonnet
2 number plate
3 queue
4 off-licence
5 single
6 pacifier
7 wash up
8 faucet
9 restroom
10 deck

## TEST 40

Number 1 is Mr Graham
Number 2 is Mr Gibson
Number 3 is Mrs Collins
Number 4 is Mr Jones
Number 5 is Father Browne
Number 6 is Mrs Gibson
Number 7 is Mrs Jones
Number 8 is Mr Collins

## TEST 41

1 borrowed
2 beside
3 building
4 fun
5 countryside
6 lying
7 taught
8 raise
9 happy
10 get up
11 bring
12 go with
13 county
14 make
15 canals
16 saving
17 check
18 work
19 rent
20 back
21 were going to
22 nice
23 invented
24 receipt
25 remind
26 fetching
27 else
28 conducted
29 grand
30 match

## TEST 42

1 borrow
2 appear
3 forget
4 take one's time
5 adore
6 praise
7 purchase /buy
8 arrive
9 decrease
10 defend
11 discourage
12 contract
13 deteriorate /get worse
14 reward
15 oppose

## TEST 43

1 planets
2 fruits
3 religions
4 buildings
5 nationalities
6 sports
7 adverbs
8 weapons
9 languages
10 vegetables
11 tools
12 weights
13 fabrics
14 jewellery
15 herbs
16 diseases
17 dances
18 prepositions
19 crimes
20 numbers

## TEST 44

| | |
|---|---|
| saloon car | 12 |
| caravan | 5 |
| van | 6 |
| hovercraft | 7 |
| submarine | 18 |
| estate car | 19 |
| articulated lorry | 1 |
| sports car | 10 |
| tanker | 11 |
| transporter | 13 |
| motorbike | 17 |
| yacht | 15 |
| coach | 20 |
| lorry | 16 |
| bus | 2 |
| barge | 9 |
| ambulance | 4 |
| taxi | 14 |
| canoe | 8 |
| tram | 3 |

## TEST 45

1 mad
2 reliable
3 amiable
4 conscious
5 immature
6 intentional
7 disgraceful
8 giddy
9 stingy
10 famished
11 absurd
12 chatty
13 pensive
14 hopeless
15 weird

## TEST 46

bear
1 hear
2 heat
3 meat
4 meal
5 seal
6 sell
7 bell
8 belt
9 bolt
10 colt
coat

## TEST 47

| | |
|---|---|
| hot water bottle | 8 |
| dummy | 14 |
| handbag | 7 |
| hamper | 15 |
| nutcracker | 12 |
| clothes rack | 3 |
| hinge | 11 |
| thimble | 2 |
| curler | 4 |
| razor blade | 10 |

tweezers  5
wallet  6
purse  13
rawlplug  9
jackplug  1

## TEST 48

1  newspaper
2  catalogue
3  atlas
4  library
5  encyclopedia
6  album
7  diary.
8  calendar
9  index
10  map
11  timetable
12  manual
13  brochure
14  directory
15  cookery book
16  dictionary
17  log
18  register

## TEST 49

1  cot, dummy
2  toothache, denture
3  sentence, judge
4  pattern, stitch
5  compartment, luggage-rack
6  filing-cabinet, typist
7  slides, snapshot ·
8  beach, deckchair
9  widow, cemetery
10  pigeon, beak
11  net, umpire
12  lapel, wear
13  bank, Danube
14  circulation, editor
15  headboard, blanket
16  bonnet, radiator
17  purr, paw
18  landing, mortgage
19  clubs, shuffle
20  prayer, hymn ("alter" is
    a verb)

## TEST 50

locket  11
alarm clock  12
stamp  13
kitchen timer  4
file  9
egg timer  7
flippers  8
pencil  15
lipstick  14
compact  2
cotton reel  5
headphones  6
identification disc  1
decanter  3
sunglasses  10

## TEST 51

1  easily
2  heavily
3  soundly
4  continuously
5  angrily
6  violently
7  deliberately
8  briefly
9  normally
10  absolutely
11  comfortably
12  patiently
13  completely
14  unexpectedly
15  fortunately/seriously
16  courageously
17  happily
18  annually
19  extremely
20  lately
21  finally
22  anxiously
23  carefully

## TEST 52

1  married
2  loyal
3  float
4  drawback
5  amble

6  blister
7  garden
8  skid
9  ache
10  deaf
11  fleas
12  enlarge
13  armpit
14  sunrise
15  alter
16  stream
17  canoe
18  crate
19  kiss
20  cheat
21  smile
22  lamp
23  melons
24  poem
25  ascend
26  chin
27  cruel
28  reward
29  evil
30  trout

## TEST 53

1  cook
2  wash
3  write
4  wear
5  listen to
6  grow
7  build
8  read
9  catch
10  deliver
11  watch
12  feed
13  play
14  fly
15  learn
16  paint
17  open
18  tie
19  drive
20  hang
21  sign
22  change
23  cross

24 celebrate
25 break
26 tell
27 run
28 lose
29 ride
30 win

## TEST 54

1 referee/whistle/match
2 decided/party/birthday
3 bird/sitting/nest
4 man/comb/pocket
5 borrowed/books/
  library
6 sofa/living-room/sales
7 chef/casserole/oven
8 woman/car/tree
9 train/platform/from
10 weather forecast/cancel/
  picnic
11 choir/song/concert
12 planets/visible/night
13 Thursday/beach/swim
14 snow/melt/sunshine
15 students/results/exams
16 those/raise/hands
17 doctor/stethoscope/
  chest
18 handwriting/terrible/
  read
19 passport/valid/countries
20 computer/invention/
  productivity

## TEST 55

1 Wrong (if they're the
  wrong colour they
  don't suit you; if they
  don't fit, they're too
  big or too small).
2 Wrong (this means you
  are big-headed and
  have a very high opin-
  ion of yourself).
3 Right (it suggests the
  person has a quick,
  clever mind).

4 Right.
5 Right (binoculars make
  distant objects seem
  closer).
6 Right (the opposite is
  voluntary).
7 Wrong (students might
  hitch-hike but they are
  very unlikely to hijack
  a plane or a train!).
8 Wrong (a timid person
  is easily frightened and
  is probably a coward).
9 Right (you would
  probably blush and feel
  very uncomfortable).
10 Right.
11 Right (it is usually
  a percentage of your
  savings).
12 Wrong (a synonym
  would be obstinate;
  mean is the opposite
  of generous).
13 Right (a ward is a room
  in a hospital for patients;
  the maternity ward is
  specially for women
  expecting babies).
14 Right (the American
  word vest is what the
  British call a waist-
  coat; this is worn over
  a shirt).
15 Wrong (you know a
  friend really well, not
  an acquaintance).
16 Right (it usually runs
  on batteries; it is sometimes called a flash-
  light).
17 Wrong (a suntan
  maybe, but they would
  hardly want to be ill
  with a fever, etc.).
18 Right (it is a type of
  hat, very common in
  France and Spain).
19 Wrong (a prune is a
  dried plum – a fruit).

20 Right (the trunk is the
  main part of a tree, a
  twig is part of a
  branch and willow is a
  type of tree).
21 Right (you pant when
  you are out of breath).
22 Wrong (most garden-
  ers try to get rid of
  weeds!).
23 Right (it looks like a
  short, thick stick).
24 Wrong (you are prob-
  ably superstitious; the
  supernatural is to do
  with ghosts and other
  things that cannot be
  explained naturally).
25 Wrong (it should be
  shade; your shadow is
  the dark shape that is
  made behind you
  when, for example, the
  sun is shining or you
  stand in front of a
  bright light).

## TEST 56

1 rich
2 sudden
3 very curious
4 clumsy
5 lazy
6 satisfied
7 uncooked
8 very old
9 lucky
10 fast
11 sleepy
12 vain
13 dependable
14 priceless
15 slight
16 fair
17 tasty
18 polite
19 faulty
20 ridiculous

## TEST 57

1 stale
2 pour
3 tease
4 suite
5 foul
6 Court
7 scene
8 doubt
9 antique
10 interfere
11 picturesque
12 decline
13 campaign
14 receipt
15 snare
16 survey
17 rehearse
18 celebrate
19 stain
20 cheer
21 yacht
22 mood

## TEST 58

1 watch
2 well
3 fence
4 change
5 faint
6 bank
7 bear
8 beat
9 blow
10 tie
11 tip
12 bridge
13 swallow
14 general
15 stamp
16 ground
17 sole
18 gum
19 season
20 lie
21 shape
22 litter
23 shell

24 match
25 ruler

## TEST 59

**Across**

1 wrist
3 salmon
6 wreck
8 guest
10 cupboard
13 gnome
14 whale
15 knight
17 thyme
19 knit
20 knee
21 calf
23 sign
25 thumb
28 bomb
29 calm
30 listen
31 dumb

**Down**

2 raspberry
4 autumn
5 numb
7 knuckle
8 gnat
9 scent
11 debt
12 palm
14 wrinkles
15 knife
16 heir
18 honest
19 knot
21 comb
22 subtle
24 ghost
26 half
27 wrong
30 lamb

## TEST 60

1 juicy
2 poisonous

3 steep
4 delicious
5 angry
6 loyal
7 sharp
8 urgent
9 deep
10 haunted
11 painful
12 stale
13 damp
14 infectious
15 lucky
16 stormy
17 parallel
18 fair
19 bumpy
20 bronze